CHILDREN'S ISSUES, LAWS AND PROGRAMS SERIES

CHILD LABOR IN AMERICA

Children's Issues, Laws and Programs Series

Federal Programs for Troubled Youth
Killian Lucero
2009. ISBN: 978-1-60692-318-4

Federal Programs for Troubled Youth
Killian Lucero
2009. ISBN: 978-1-60876-701-4
(Online book)

Child Sexual Abuse: Pitfalls in the Substantiation Process
Anna Aprile, Cristina Ranzato, Melissa Rosa Rizzotto and Paola Facchin
2009. ISBN: 978-1-60741-427-8

Diet Quality of American Young Children
Calvin G. Parker (Editor)
2009. ISBN: 978-1-60692-771-7

Diet Quality of American School-Age Children
Kelly B. Volkarsky (Editor)
2009. ISBN: 978-1-60692-776-2

National School Lunch Program Assessment
Manuel P. Borges (Editor)
2009. ISBN: 978-1-60692-972-8

Reading First Impact Study
Beth C. Games , Howard S. Bloom, James J. Kemple, Robin Tepper Jacob, Beth Boulay, Laurie Bozzi, Linda Caswell, Megan Horst, W. Carter Smith, Robert G. St.Pierre, Fatih Unlu, Corinne Herlihy and Pei Zhu
2009. ISBN: 978-1-60741-529-9

Vulnerable and Disconnected Youth: Background and Policies
Dierk Neumann (Editor)
2010 ISBN: 978-1-60741-488-9

Foster Care and African-American Youth
Joanna Kaczmarek (Editor)
2010 ISBN: 978-1-60741-541-1

Preschool Children: Physical Activity, Behavioral Assessment and Developmental Challenges
Leone Colombo and Rachele Bianchi
2010 ISBN: 978-1-60876-026-8

Child Development and Child Poverty
Anselm Fiedler and Isidor Kuester
2010 ISBN: 978-1-60741-816-0

Child Protection, the Courts and Social Workers
Terrance R. Langely (Editor)
2010 ISBN: 978-1-60741-279-3

Child Labor in America
Ian C. Rivera and Natasha M. Howard (Editor)
2010 ISBN: 978-1-60876-769-4

Adam W alsh Child Protection and Safety Act: Analysis and Law
Terrell G. Sandoval (Editor)
2010 ISBN: 978-1-61668-808-0

Adam Walsh Child Protection and Safety Act: Analysis and Law
Terrell G. Sandoval (Editor)
2010 ISBN: 978-1-61668-878-3
(Online book)

When Abuse and Neglect Occur at Residential Treatment Facilities
Kirsten S. Madsen (Editor
2010 ISBN: 978-1-60876-965-0

Child Abduction Resources
Melanie H. Wilson (Editor)
2010 ISBN: 978-1-61668-247-7

Working with the Courts in Child Protection
Raymond T. Devon (Editor)
2010 ISBN: 978-1-61668-303-0

Working with the Courts in Child Protection
Raymond T. Devon (Editor)
2010 ISBN: 978-1-61668-426-6
(Online book)

CHILDREN'S ISSUES, LAWS AND PROGRAMS SERIES

CHILD LABOR IN AMERICA

IAN C. RIVERA
AND
NATASHA M. HOWARD
EDITORS

Nova Science Publishers, Inc.
New York

For permission to use material from this book please contact us:
Telephone 631-231-7269; Fax 631-231-8175
Web Site: http://www.novapublishers.com

LIBRARY OF CONGRESS CATALOGING-IN-PUBLICATION DATA

Child labor in America / editors, Ian C. Rivera and Natasha M. Howard.
p. cm.
Includes index.
ISBN 978-1-60876-769-4 (softcover)
1. Child labor--United States. 2. Child labor--Government policy--United States. 3. Child labor--Law and legislation--United States. I. Rivera, Ian C. II. Howard, Natasha M.
HD6250.U3C443 2009
331.3'10973--dc22
2009046486

Published by Nova Science Publishers, Inc. † New York

CONTENTS

PREFACE

The history of child labor in America is long and, in some cases, unsavory. It dates back to the founding of the United States. Traditionally, most children, except for the privileged few, had always worked - either for their parents or for an outside employer. Through the years, however, child labor practices have changed. So have the benefits and risks associated with employment of children. In some respects, altered workplace technology has served to make work easier and less hazardous. At the same time, some processes and equipment have rendered the workplace more dangerous, especially for children and youth. This book examines the current state of enforcement of America's federal child labor laws by the Department of Labor. This historical issue of child labor in America is also briefly reviewed. In addition, recommendations are made about reforms to strengthen protections for working children from hazardous working conditions. This book consists of public documents which have been located, gathered, combined, reformatted, and enhanced with a subject index, selectively edited and bound to provide easy access.

Chapters 1 through 5 feature testimony before the U. S. House of Representatives.

Chapter 6 - The history of child labor in America is long and, in some cases, unsavory. It dates back to the founding of the United States. Traditionally, most children, except for the privileged few, had always worked — either for their parents or for an outside employer. Through the years, however, child labor practices have changed. So have the benefits and risks associated with employment of children. In some respects, altered workplace technology has served to make work easier and less hazardous. At the same time, some processes and equipment have rendered the workplace more dangerous, especially for children and youth.

In: Child Labor in America
Ed: I. C. Rivera and N. M. Howard
ISBN: 978-1-60876-769-4

Chapter 1

CHILD LABOR ENFORCEMENT HEARING: TESTIMONY OF NORMA FLORES TO THE HOUSE EDUCATION AND LABOR COMMITTEE'S SUBCOMMITTE ON WORKFORCE PROTECTIONS

Norma Flores

My name is Norma Flores and I am just one of estimated hundreds of thousands of farmworker children working hard to feed Americans every day. My four sisters and I began to work in the farm fields since the age of 12 during our summers and any other school breaks we had, but we weren't strangers to farm work at that age. Full-time work weeks now meant 70 hours — including weekends — for weeks at a time with no days off. Growing up in a family of many generations of farm workers, we thought life was supposed to be this hard for everyone. Even though we saw both of our parents work hard year-round and spend every penny carefully, we grew up poor. This taught us to value all of our possessions differently. We knew if we wanted a nice pair of sneakers or a ticket to see a new movie, those would be things that would have to be earned with a lot of hard hours of difficult manual labor.

But this was life to us. We weren't informed of what rights we had or educated on what resources were available to help us. In the six years that I worked in the fields, I never saw an inspector in any of the fields I was working in. Had I seen an inspector out there, I would have pointed out the lack of clean bathrooms sometimes half a mile away and the lack of places to wash our hands after handling plants covered in pesticides. I would have pointed out the missing drinking water and the containers with day-old water we had to drink from at times. I would have pointed out the under-age children allowed to work during regular school hours. Working in the corn fields of Indiana or in the asparagus fields of Michigan, it felt like we were at the mercy of the contractors with no one to look out for us and no one to turn to for questions or concerns. One of the most terrifying moments of my life was when an airplane accidently sprayed pesticides over the field my family and I were working in. We ran out frantically across the street and immediately called our contractor. He simply apologized and asked us to go to another field to continue our work day. Who were we supposed to contact in case we got sick from the pesticides? How would we know?

Farm labor is difficult and dangerous work. We are exposed to many chemicals that can damage our health and migrant farmworkers don't have benefits like health insurance to help us with expensive medical treatments. We are exposed to long hours in hot summer months with back-breaking labor. We work with sharp tools and heavy machinery that can cause a lot of damage if not used properly. Yet as children, we are trusted to have the ability and maturity to handle all of these dangers carefully. I have seen too many times accidents in which children working beside me have gotten deeply cut and infected with the sharp tools we work with or sick from the chemicals we work around. Children at age 12 would not have been allowed to work making copies in an air-conditioned office or cleaning floors at a local store, yet today, in America, children can legally work in harsh conditions out in the farm fields for wages sometimes below minimum wage.

Like all other Americans across the country, the migrant community is also concerned about today's economy. We see in the news how gas prices and the cost of living are on the rise. Yet what we don't see rising are our wages. Since Cesar Chavez, no major improvements in the lives of migrant farmworkers have been made. They continue to receive the same pay as decades ago. Growers claim that wages must be kept low in order for food prices to stay affordable, but at what price? Is it worth it to exploit children and hurt their futures so you won't have to pay cents more for your groceries? Even this isn't saving Americans from the rising food price inflation. By giving fair wages, migrant families will no longer need their children to work to supplement their incomes and these farmworker children can focus on their studies instead of worrying about the pending family bills.

I was blessed to have parents that put my education as a top priority and migrant youth programs that helped give the educational support I needed to get through my education. After overcoming many educational hardships including interrupted school years and different state school systems, I was able to graduate from one of the nation s leading high schools and complete college in three and a half years. Even though my family continues to work in the fields of Iowa and Texas, I proudly work in an international public relations firm in downtown Chicago.

Other farmworker children aren't so fortunate. I believe that at least two-thirds of migrant farmworker children drop out before high school graduation from the pressures of migration, changing schools, and exhaustion. This dooms most of them to a life of poverty.

Farmworker children continue to be an ignored injustice today in the United States, the worlds greatest country. The information is out there, but many choose to look the other way. Just Google migrant farmworker children and youll get over 87,000 results. Exploitation of children, regardless if it s done legally or illegally, needs to stop today. Its more than doing what is right. Its also about changing the lives of these children and giving them the opportunity to make a future for themselves.

In: Child Labor in America
Ed: I. C. Rivera and N. M. Howard
ISBN: 978-1-60876-769-4

Chapter 2

CHILD LABOR ENFORCEMENT HEARING: TESTIMONY BY SALLY GREENBERG

Sally Greenberg
National Consumers League

Thank you for inviting me to testify today. My name is Sally Greenberg, and I serve as Executive Director of the National Consumers League. We very much appreciate the Subcommittee on Workforce Protections holding a hearing that asks, "Child Labor Enforcement: Are We Adequately Protecting our Children?" The National Consumers League believes that that answer to the question this Subcommittee hearing poses is "No," and that much more can and must be done to better protect our young people from hazards and dangers they confront in the workplace.[1]

Every 10 days in America, a young person is killed at work. Every day, more than 100 young workers under the age of 19 are seriously injured or become ill from their jobs.

My testimony today focuses on the U.S. Department of Labor, or DOL's poor enforcement of the federal child labor laws and I will make recommendations about reforms I would like to see at DOL to strengthen protections for working children. I will also make recommendations for legislative reforms that we believe Congress should consider to help to protect our young people from hazardous work conditions.

The National Consumers League, or "NCL," is a private, non-profit advocacy group representing consumers on marketplace and workplace issues.

Our mission is to protect and promote social and economic justice for consumers and workers in the United States and abroad. We are the nation's oldest consumer organization. The NCL is the co-chair, along with the American Federation of Teachers, of the Child Labor Coalition, or "CLC." The CLC, established in 1989, is a group of more than 30 organizations, representing consumers, labor unions, educators, human rights and labor rights groups, child advocacy groups, and religious and women's groups. The CLC's mission is to protect working youth and to promote legislation, programs, and initiatives to end child labor exploitation in the United States and abroad.

Let me start by saying that the NCL very much supports the notion young people can learn and grow by working, as long as they are placed in a jobs that are appropriate and safe. We wish to focus, however, on workplace settings and jobs that are risky or dangerous for young people and what can be done to correct the loopholes in the law that expose youngsters to these workplace hazards.

Much of my testimony is based on the findings of two reports on DOL's child labor enforcement released by the Child Labor Coalition and published by the National Consumers League, one in June 2005 and the other in September 2006, as well as more recent data on the same topic. I have provided copies of the two reports to the Subcommittee, and I ask that they be included in the record.

What these reports make clear is that enforcement of the child labor law is no longer a high priority for DOL.

Here is a quick overview that shows why this is so.

- First, *the number of child labor investigations by DOL has declined drastically*. For example, there was a 48 percent decline from 2004 to 2006 — 2,606 child labor investigations in 2004, but only 1,344 in 2006.[2] If we look back more than two years, the story is even worse. The number of child labor investigations conducted in 2006 — 1,344 — was the lowest in the last ten years for which we have data, and may be the lowest in many decades.
- Second, the time spent investigating child labor also declined: 58,220 hours in 2004, but only 48,005 hours in 2006. If we look back more than two years, the story is even worse. For example, from 2001, when the Wage-Hour division spent 73,736 hours doing child labor investigations, to 2006, the time devoted to child labor investigations plummeted by 35 percent. The 48,005 hours spent by DOL in 2006 investigating child labor violations may sound like a lot of time, but

based on our calculations, this is roughly the equivalent of 28 full-time employees doing child labor investigations exclusively.[3] There are an estimated 3.2 million working children in the United States, according to the federal government.[4] In other words, each of these 28 DOL child labor investigators is in effect responsible for assuring a safe and healthy work environment for about 115,000 youth workers.

- Third, *the penalties that DOL imposes are too low to provide sufficient deterrent to companies hiring underage workers*. While the law imposes a maximum penalty of $11,000 for each violation,[5] the average penalty in 2004 was only $718, less than 7 percent of the maximum penalty permitted. Two years later, in 2006, the average penalty was only $939, less than 9 percent of the maximum penalty. Here's a concrete example of low child labor penalties. In 2006 DOL found 29 children in six Target Corporation retail stores in New York's Hudson River Valley who had been working in jobs prohibited for children under age 18 because the work is so hazardous—operating power-driver scrap paper balers and operating power-driven hoisting equipment, like forklifts.[6] DOL imposed a penalty of $92,400, or an average of $3,166 per child, not a lot for a multibillion dollar corporation. Another example dates from 2005. Wal-Mart committed child labor violations affecting 85 children in 24 stores, many involving youth who did jobs that DOL has determined to be particularly dangerous, such as operating chain saws, cardboard balers, and forklifts.[7] DOL imposed $135,540 in penalties, or an average of $1,595 per child. Given that Wal-Mart had $285 billion in annual sales, the $135,540 total penalty is a negligible amount—the equivalent of fining someone with an average salary a tiny fraction of a penny. The law says that the size of any child labor penalty that DOL imposes must take account of "the size of the business of the person charged and the gravity of the violation,"[8] but it is hard to see how DOL has done that in its investigations, given the very low amount of the average penalty imposed.
- Fourth, *DOL has almost no child labor enforcement in agriculture.* Hundreds of thousands of children work in agriculture, yet, in 2006, just 28 of DOL's 1,344 child labor investigations—2 percent—were in agriculture. In 2005 the number of child labor investigations in agriculture was even lower—just 25. These numbers contrast sharply with earlier years. In 1999, for example, DOL conducted more than five times as many investigations in agriculture—142. What is

particularly troubling about this poor enforcement record is that the risks of injury, illness, and death are greater for children working in agriculture than in any other jobs. For example, children age 15 to 17 working in agriculture have over four times the risk of fatal injury of children working in other industries.[9] Children under age 15 working on farms account for about three-fourths of all work-related deaths for that age group.[10] As for nonfatal injuries, hospital emergency room and workers' compensation data have suggested that youth injuries in agriculture tend to be more severe than injuries in other employments.[11]

What can DOL do to assure greater protections to working children? There are several key steps DOL should take.

- First, *DOL needs to devote more time and effort to investigating potential child labor violations.* The equivalent of 28 full-time child labor investigators for the entire United States is simply indefensible. The child labor provisions of the FLSA are unique in that only DOL can enforce them, whereas the FLSA's minimum wage and overtime pay provisions can be enforced not only by DOL, but also by aggrieved employees represented by lawyers in court. In other words, if DOL places less emphasis on enforcing the minimum wage and overtime pay provisions, employees have another route to address the problem—a private right of action.. In 2006, for example, DOL filed only 3 percent—143 of 4,207— FLSA lawsuits in federal court. But if DOL does not enforce the FLSA's child labor provisions, then no one else can.
- Second, *DOL needs to impose much higher penalties than in the past.* Average penalties of less than $1,000 do not provide sufficient deterrent effect. There is no deterrent effect when a large company faces a nominal penalty after permitting underage youth to perform work forbidden under DOL regulations. DOL could easily change its regulations, or even just revise its internal procedures for calculating penalties, to achieve this result. Moreover, DOL should take employers who commit repeat child labor violations to court to get an injunction barring future violations, as the FLSA authorizes DOL to do. Any employer that violates such an injunction can be held in contempt of court and be required to pay DOL's costs of investigating

and prosecuting to prove to the court that the employer has violated the injunction.

- Third, *DOL needs to update and strengthen its regulations* that list jobs that are so hazardous that no child under age 18 (or in agriculture, under age 16) can do them. The government's premier job safety agency—the National Institute for Occupational Safety and Health, or "NIOSH"— issued a lengthy report over six years ago recommending that more than half of these existing regulations be revised and that 17 new regulations be added, but DOL has acted on a paltry number of these recommendations, and adopted no changes whatsoever for agriculture, the most dangerous work environment for children. Six years of inaction, while children are maimed and injured on the job, are six years too many. DOL's refusal to protect working children by appropriately revising the hazardous orders is inexcusable.
- Fourth, DOL needs to conduct targeted investigations of two industries in which child laborers may be most vulnerable to death or injury: agriculture and meatpacking. It has been nearly a decade since the Department of Labor's targeted Salad Bowl investigation found dozens of children, including many under the age of 10, helping harvest the nation's fruits and vegetables. And in the area of slaughterhouses, the recent investigation by the State of Iowa of the Agriprocessors plant in Postville, Iowa found dozens of minors working illegally in what is often considered to be one of the worst and most dangerous jobs in America. In August, NCL spoke to an Agriprocessors child laborer who had stabbed himself in the arm while on the cutting line and had been bandaged up and told to go back to work. The young worker said he was routinely cheated out of hours of wages each week. He also said that he believed his plant supervisors knew he was too young to work in the plant but looked the other way. Given that meat processing plants tend to attract an impoverished, mostly immigrant work force, the possibility that child laborers may be employed in slaughterhouse around the nation should be investigated by U.S. DOL with vigor.
- Fifth, *DOL needs to publicize its child labor enforcement activities much more aggressively.* The most that DOL does typically is to issue an innocuous press release, and in many instances no publicity at all is given to child labor penalty cases. This approach needs to be changed drastically to make both employers and employees much more aware

of the child labor laws, and the penalties that can result for violating those laws.

- Sixth, DOL needs to revive the Child Labor Task Force that coordinated child labor enforcement efforts between state and federal inspectors. Increased coordination and communication between state and federal inspectors should increase the efficacy of enforcement efforts.

What can this Committee and Congress do to strengthen the child labor law? We have several recommendations:

- First, Congress must increase funding for DOL Wage and Hour inspectors. One of the primary reasons for the lack of child labor enforcement: Wage and Hour is grossly understaffed. Less than 750 investigators are available to go out into the field and investigate labor violations. That translates to one investigator for every 10,000 businesses. Kim Bobo, the executive director of Interfaith Worker Justice testified in Congress earlier this summer, that if the ratio of investigators to businesses that existed in 1941 held today, we would have 34,000 investigators—not less than 1,000. As a first step, NCL believes the number of inspectors should be doubled and Congress should mandate that child labor inspections become a greater priority of enforcement efforts. Congress should require DOL to report on its enhanced child labor enforcement efforts not less than 18 months after funding for the additional inspectors is provided.
- Second, *Congress should eliminate many of the special exclusions in agriculture* that permit children as young as young as 12 years old, and in some cases even younger, to work in the fields. It is unconscionable to allow 12 year olds to toil in over 100 degree heat and be exposed to toxic chemicals and pesticides; this gaping loophole in the law should be changed. By doing so, Congress would ensure that children working in agriculture would be subject to the same protections as children working in all other jobs. We are not talking here about children who work on their own parent's farms (who are not subject to the child labor law at all), but children who work for hire on farms, such as migrant and seasonal farmworkers. Rep. Lucille Roybal-Allard's "Childrens Act for Responsible Employment," also known as the CARE Act, would close these shameful loopholes, leveling the playing field for hundreds of

thousands of farmworker youth who are dropping out of high school in high numbers.

- Third, because of the great hazards to children working in agriculture, *Congress should strengthen the protections for children working on farms.* Under existing law, the Secretary of Labor has the authority to declare which jobs are particularly hazardous for children, and the law provides a minimum age of 18 for such jobs—except in agriculture, where the minimum age is 16. For example, a young worker must be 18 to drive a forklift at a Wal-Mart warehouse, but that young worker could drive a forklift at a fruit and vegetable packing house at age 16—even though the dangers are very similar.
- Congress should amend the law to raise the minimum age for doing particularly hazardous work in agriculture to 18, especially in view of the high incidence of deaths and injuries to children working in agriculture (as noted above). The CARE Act would remedy this problem as well.
- Fourth, *Congress should impose minimum penalties for child labor violations* —say at $500—to make employers more likely to comply with the child labor requirements.

Thank you again, Madam Chair, for calling this hearing on whether young workers are being properly protected in America's workplace. The National Consumers League remains ready to work with you and your staff to see that children in this country are kept safe and are protected against the many dangers and hazards they may face in the workplace.

End Notes

[1]

[2] The data we have are based on the federal fiscal year, not the calendar year. Also, our data go only through 2006, because information on DOL's child labor enforcement is not on the DOL Web site; the data are available through a Freedom of Information Act request only – we have filed a FOIA request but have yet to receive the information.

[3] A full-time DOL employee with a 40-hour workweek for 52 weeks is paid for 2,080 hours per year, but with time off for vacations, holidays, and sick leave for medical appointments and illnesses, actual working hours in a year are probably closer to 1,700 hours. Thus, the 48,005 child labor investigative hours in 2006 would require the equivalent of about 28 full-time employees.

[4] The National Institute for Occupational Safety and Health (NIOSH), relying on reports by DOL's Bureau of Labor Statistics and the Current Population Survey, estimates that 2.78 million 16- and 17-year-old children were employed in 2000, as well as over 450,000 15-

year-olds, for a total of 3,230,000 youth workers. *National Institute for Occupational Safety and Health (NIOSH) Recommendations to the U.S. Department of Labor for Changes to Hazardous Orders* (May 2002), p. 3 ("NIOSH Report") (available at www.cdc.gov/niosh/docs/NIOSHR ecsDOLHaz/ DOL-recomm.pdf). The NIOSH Report has no estimate for the number of youth workers under age 15. However, many children under this age do in fact work, as evidenced by DOL's Bureau of Labor Statistics estimate that 134 children under age 15 were killed on the job during the period 1992-1998 (see report on the Youth Work Force, revised November 2000, Chapter 6, p. 60 (Table 6.1), available at www.bls.gov/opub/rylf/pdf.

[5] This $11,000 maximum penalty was increased by FLSA child labor amendments included in the Genetic Information Nondiscrimination Act, or "GINA" (which took effect on May 21, 2008), with regard to particularly serious child labor violations. Any child labor violation that causes death or serious injury now has a maximum penalty of $50,000, which can be doubled where the violation is a repeated or willful violation. We don't know whether DOL has begun to impose these higher penalties, though they took effect over four months ago.

[6] The information about the Target Corporation child labor investigation comes from the *Daily Labor Report* of April 19, 2006, published by the Bureau of National Affairs in Washington, D.C.

[7] The information about the Wal-Mart child labor investigation is based largely on articles in The New York Times on February 12 and 21, 2005.

[8] FLSA section 16(e), 29 U.S.C. 216(e).

[9] *National Institute for Occupational Safety and Health (NIOSH Recommendations to the U.S. Department of Labor for Changes in Hazardous Orders* (U.S. Department of Health and Human services, Public health Service, Centers for Disease Control and Prevention, May 2002), p.12, available at http://www.cdc.gov/niosh/docs/NIOSHRecsDOLHaz/default.html.

[10] Ibid.

[11] Id. at p. 7.

In: Child Labor in America
Ed: I. C. Rivera and N. M. Howard
ISBN: 978-1-60876-769-4

Chapter 3

CHILD LABOR ENFORCEMENT: ARE WE ADEQUATELY PROTECTING OUR CHILDREN?

Alexander J. Passantino
Wage and Hour Division, U.S. Dept. of Labor

Chairwoman Woolsey, Ranking Member Wilson, and distinguished members of the Subcommittee

Thank you for the opportunity to discuss the efforts taken by the Department of Labor's (Department) Wage and Hour Division (WHD) to promote compliance with the Fair Labor Standard Act's (FLSA) child labor provisions. Let me begin by saying that WHD is committed to full and fair enforcement of all the laws under WHD's jurisdiction, but WHD staff's dedication to ensuring that youth in this country work safely and legally is second to none. As I will highlight, our accomplishments in strengthening child labor laws, raising public awareness of child labor requirements, and targeting industries in which young workers are likely to be injured or killed on the job have contributed to safer workplaces for young workers.

Like all regulatory enforcement agencies, WHD employs a variety of tools and activities to enforce the law and achieve compliance. The agency's mission is to *promote and achieve compliance*—not just to identify violations after they occur, but particularly in instances in which the health and safety of workers are concerned, to prevent violations in the first instance. The agency's child labor activities and initiatives are far too numerous to list individually, so I will point out our key efforts and accomplishments over the past several years.

WHD Enforcement Priorities In Improving Child Labor Compliance

WHD has prioritized its statutory enforcement responsibilities to maximize protections for the greatest number of workers, including those most vulnerable in the workforce—low-wage workers, immigrants, and *young workers*. The absence of a private right of action to address oppressive child labor underscores the importance of this agency's role in safeguarding young workers. For this reason, increasing compliance with the child labor provisions of the FLSA is a cornerstone of the agency's annual performance plan. Every on-site investigation—complaint or directed—has a child labor component. Every low wage initiative—targeted for child labor compliance or targeted for other compliance reasons—requires that investigators examine child labor compliance. Child labor complaints, although not numerous, are given the highest priority within the agency. Every WHD investigator is trained early in his or her career to look for child labor violations. With each national child labor initiative, investigators gain both a renewed focus and specialized training.

Each year, WHD regional and local offices plan and undertake child labor compliance initiatives in a variety of industries and businesses, such as grocery stores, shopping malls, theaters, and restaurants. These industries are among those in which the agency has historically found high levels of non-compliance with the child labor Hazardous Occupations Orders (HOs) and in which large numbers of young workers are traditionally employed. The agency's low-wage initiatives in other industries, such as construction and agriculture, also require district offices to examine an employer's compliance with the FLSA child labor provisions in conjunction with a minimum wage or overtime investigation or concomitant with the labor standards statutes that apply to agricultural workers.

In recent fiscal years, WHD regional and district offices have developed child labor compliance initiatives in industries or establishments that had a history of child labor HO violations or that have a high likelihood that a young employee might suffer a work-related injury or fatality. In fiscal year 2006, for example, WHD offices nationwide investigated discount department store operations to determine the level of compliance with the child labor provisions, in particular to determine their compliance with HOs that regulate paper balers, forklifts, and teen driving. In fiscal year 2007, district and regional offices continued their emphasis on reducing injuries and deaths to young workers by stressing compliance with the HOs. This year, the agency placed a particular emphasis on increasing compliance with HO No. 12, which regulates the loading and operating paper balers and compactors—a common and particularly hazardous piece of equipment found in many retail establishments and increasingly used in nursing homes, schools, and restaurants. The focus on HO No. 12 compliance will continue in fiscal year 2009 as offices develop their child labor initiatives for the upcoming fiscal year.

Several key statistics support the agency's continued emphasis on child labor enforcement. First, the number of enforcement hours charged to child labor compliance has averaged 57,900 over the last seven years (from fiscal year 2001 through fiscal year 2007). This is not significantly different than the 58,080 average child labor enforcement hours recorded during the preceding seven years (from fiscal year 1994 through fiscal year 2000).

Second, as noted above, WHD investigators examine child labor compliance in all on-site investigations. In the last three years, approximately 47 percent of the investigations in which a child labor violation was identified occurred in an on-site investigation initiated under another statute or program area enforced by WHD— primarily in investigations initiated to determine FLSA minimum wage and overtime compliance.

Third, the percentage of child labor cases in which a child labor violation is found has increased steadily over the last three years. Thirty-seven percent of child labor investigations in fiscal year 2005 found child labor violations. By the end of fiscal year 2007, the percentage had increased to 40 percent, which suggests improvements in targeting establishments and industries with likely child labor violations.

Fourth, WHD civil money penalty assessments per investigation have increased from $4,558 assessed per case in fiscal year 2003 to $5,303 assessed per case in fiscal year 2007. The agency has not hesitated to levy fines against employers found in violation of the child labor laws—proportionate to the severity of the violations. Although we have been successful in collecting civil money penalties, as established in the examples below, the more significant and long-term results have been demonstrated in our ability to secure future corporate-wide compliance and cooperative public awareness campaigns by many of the investigated companies. Recent investigations include the following examples:

- In August 2008, American Multi-Cinema, Inc., (AMC Theatres), headquartered in Kansas City, Missouri, paid $141,570 in child labor civil money penalties to resolve violations found in AMC theaters in several states. As part of the resolution, AMC Theaters produced a child labor public service announcement (PSA) on hazards associated with compactors and balers. The PSA is being shown in theatres nationwide as part of the company's *First Look* pre-feature entertainment program, and the expected audience is 8 million theater-goers.
- In January 2008, the Department obtained a permanent injunction in U.S. district court against Paragon Contractors Corp., a Hildale, Utah, contractor, for repeated violations of federal youth employment laws. The most recent investigation uncovered a 16-year-old working in roofing operations in violation of HO No. 16. The assessed civil money penalty of $5,280 was paid by the company.
- In December 2007, Connecticut-based CVS Pharmacy Inc. agreed to pay $226,598 in child labor civil money penalties after a 2007 investigation of CVS stores in New England and the Mid-Atlantic states found 78 minors illegally loading, unloading, or operating cardboard compactors and seven minors employed in violation of the FLSA time standards. CVS Pharmacy Inc. also agreed to ensure compliance with the FLSA at its more than 6,000 stores nationwide.
- In July 2007, Pretzel King LLC, doing business as an Auntie Anne's franchisee in San Bernardino, Downey, Arcadia, Glendale, Northridge and Bakersfield, California, paid $51,500 in civil monetary penalties for allowing eleven 14- and 15-year-olds to work beyond the hours permitted by law and nine youths to be involved in prohibited baking activities. The stores also allowed 60 minors to operate freight elevators, dough mixers, and trash compactors, which are prohibited hazardous occupations for anyone under 18 years of age.
- In 2007, Jim Barnes Enterprises Inc., a McDonald's franchisee, paid $86,500 in penalties after WHD determined that the firm allowed minors to perform hazardous duties, *e.g.*, operating a trash compactor and frying, at a Mobile, Alabama, restaurant. In addition, a Piggly Wiggly franchisee, SCVS Inc., paid $30,000 in penalties after an investigation found 20 minors operating paper balers at two stores.

These violations were uncovered as part of the WHD's Gulf Coast District Office local child labor initiative to increase compliance in grocery stores and restaurants.

- In the summer of 2007, Caesars Utah LLC, doing business as Little Caesars Pizza in Sandy, Utah, paid a $110,800 civil monetary penalty for allowing minors to operate dough mixers and bake, among other activities in violation of the child labor provisions. The company also agreed to educate the public at large by creating a statewide public service campaign called *Stop, Look and Listen.*
- In April 2006, Target Corporation paid $92,400 in civil money penalties for exposing young workers to hazardous machinery in violation of the FLSA child labor provisions. Twenty-nine minors in seven New York/New Jersey-area stores were found to have operated either power-driven hoisting apparatus or power- driven scrap paper balers, or in some cases, both. The company provided WHD with an outline of the steps it planned to take to ensure full compliance with all child labor regulations in the future.

WHD believes its continued emphasis on child labor compliance has resulted in fewer child labor violations. The total number of investigations in which child labor violations were found is lower today than the total number in 2001, and the trend appears to be continuing. The number of minors found illegally employed last fiscal year (4,672) is nearly half of the number found illegally employed in fiscal year 2001 (8,818). The average number of minors found illegally employed per investigation has also declined from 4.2 in fiscal year 2001 to 3.7 in fiscal year 2007. More importantly, the number of minors found employed in violation of a hazardous occupations order in fiscal year 2007 (1,000) was a reduction of more than half the number found working in a hazardous situation in fiscal year 2001 (2,040). While these statistics can be attributed in part to the overall drop in the number of teens in the workplace, these declining trends should also be taken as an encouraging sign that fewer young workers are employed in violation of the law.

Children who work in agriculture are among the most vulnerable of the country's workers. The nature of agricultural employment, *i.e.*, its short duration, the remote locations, and mobility of the work, pose particular enforcement challenges. Agricultural work is difficult and dangerous. For youth, the hazards are significant. The fatality rate for young workers in agriculture is nearly six times the rate in other industries. Nearly 60 percent of the youth fatalities in agriculture during 1998—2002 occurred to youths whc

worked on the family farms. The deaths of young family farm workers accounted for nearly a quarter of all of the young worker deaths that occurred in all industries during the same period.

The standards for youth employment in agriculture have historically differed from nonagricultural employment. Under the FLSA, the child of a farmer can do any job, at any age, at any time, on a farm owned or operated by the parent of that child. The minimum age for employment is lower than for nonagricultural work. There is no minimum age for employment on small farms that the Act exempts from minimum wage requirements. The agricultural HOs prohibit only those youth under the age of 16, who are *not* working on his or her own family farm, from performing those tasks that the Secretary has found to be particularly hazardous for youth, as opposed to nonagricultural HOs, which apply to youth under the age of 18. Because youth are permitted to work in agriculture at a younger age, WHD is committed to promoting their safe employment in the industry. WHD investigators who conduct investigations in the agricultural industry are instructed to examine compliance with the provisions of all applicable statutes providing protections for agricultural workers, particularly wages, housing, and transportation, field worker safety and *child labor* provisions. WHD investigated four occupational fatalities that occurred in fiscal years 2007 and 2008 involving teens under the age of 16 working in agriculture. Of those four cases, WHD found that only one involved a violation of the FLSA child labor provisions. The employer was assessed $11,962 in civil money penalties—the maximum allowable penalty at the time. In the remaining three instances, there was no employment relationship.

Even in situations in which young workers are not subject to the FLSA child labor provisions, WHD has looked to methods other than enforcement to help young farm workers on family farms enjoy safe and positive work experiences. As I will discuss later, WHD has developed compliance assistance materials emphasizing occupational safety and health, disseminated public service announcements, and collaborated with other entities to educate parents and teens of "age-appropriate" task standards that parents can use to measure the capabilities of their children in performing agricultural work.

Compliance Assistance and Public Awareness Campaigns Affect Compliance

Compliance assistance activities, which include providing clear and easy-toaccess information on how to comply with federal employment laws, are key strategies in promoting voluntary compliance and should not be discounted. Parents, educators, employers, and young workers who are aware of the federal and state child labor requirements can make more informed decisions on when and where young people should work. Compliance assistance and educational activities are communicated in many ways, whether through speeches and presentations given to school groups or by PSAs. WHD uses every available means to provide compliance information to the public. WHD staff speak regularly to employer, employee, community, and advocacy groups. Local offices distribute self-audit materials and compliance guides to help employers evaluate their employment practices against the child labor laws. WHD investigators and managers work directly with school and work-permit officials to educate issuing authorities on how to screen potential violations before the work actually begins. With over 7 million covered worksites in the U.S., voluntary compliance with the child labor laws must be encouraged and supported.

In May 2002, the Department launched the *YouthRules!* public awareness campaign, which quickly became the centerpiece of WHD's child labor compliance and public awareness efforts. The *YouthRules!* initiative is designed to increase public awareness of both federal and state rules concerning young workers; since its implementation, the initiative has provided an easily recognizable vehicle by which the public can obtain compliance materials. The web page, www.youthrules.dol.gov, provides a gateway to child labor compliance information on the internet. The site gets approximately 500,000 views a year in part because some 75 partners, associations, and governmental entities have linked or agreed to link their web site to the *YouthRules!* site. Most recently, Major League Baseball established an internet link from its web site to the agency's *YouthRules!* page.

As part of this public awareness effort, WHD published and distributed a *YouthRules!* bookmarks and a *YouthRules! Employer Pocket Guide* in both English and Spanish. Similar publications were developed to educate employers and the public about the rules for youth employment in agriculture. Each year, WHD augments these printed and on-line *YouthRules!* materials with new fact sheets, guides, and other aides for compliance. WHD developed and posted self-assessment tools for restaurants, grocery stores, and other non-agricultural industries to help employers assess their compliance with the child labor laws. WHD designed posters with bold attention-getting colors and graphics to attract young readers. Agency field personnel developed a child labor compliance PowerPoint presentation geared towards a teenaged audience. The *YouthRules!* web site contains stickers that employers may place on dangerous equipment to warn teens and others that young workers are not permitted to operate certain equipment, such as forklifts and paper balers. Wage and Hour regularly updates this website to inform the public of new developments, such as the publication of new regulations.

The Department also developed and disseminated a *YouthRules!* PSA in fiscal year 2004. That first year, over 6,000 radio stations received a taped PSA, and 10,000 newspapers received a *YouthRules!* news article, including ethnic media and newspapers. That year, the radio PSA played over 340 times on 197 radio stations with an audience of 27 million listeners in 39 states. The print article generated 252 newspaper articles in 20 states with a readership of approximately 15 million.

In fiscal years 2005 and 2006, WHD's summer public awareness campaign focused on youth employed in construction, because of increasing numbers of young workers—primarily Hispanic—employed in that industry. As part of the campaign, WHD launched a new electronic seminar, "*Youth Working in Construction,*" which is available on CD-ROM and on the *YouthRules!* web site. The seminar discusses the requirements for youth working in construction and concentrates on identifying the prohibited occupations in construction. A radio PSA and print article were issued to highlight the new seminar.

WHD's first *YouthRules!* rally was held in 2003. The event, at a Philadelphia mall, was highly successful, so WHD expanded the concept in 2004 to include additional rallies in Houston and New Jersey. The rallies are now annual events in Houston and San Antonio. Participation in the events numbers in the thousands.

In the last fiscal year, WHD updated the child labor PSAs and distributed them to more than 1,900 radio stations, including all 600 Spanish radio stations in the U.S. and Puerto Rico. The new PSAs focused on youth in agriculture—the industry with the highest youth fatality rate. WHD continued public dissemination of the PSAs as part of this year's annual *YouthRules!* campaign.

These diverse public awareness and compliance assistance activities continue a longstanding WHD tradition of promoting positive and safe work experiences by educating parents, teens, employers, educators, and the public at large about the federal and state rules concerning young workers. The goal, as stated earlier, is to increase compliance and prevent violations from occurring in the first instance and through those efforts, safeguard the lives and futures of young workers.

PARTNERSHIPS PROMOTE CHILD LABOR COMPLIANCE

Strategic partnerships provide opportunities and avenues to encourage compliance in communities and among employers. Business associations, unions, state governments, federal agencies, community groups, academia, and others have collaborated with WHD to promote public awareness and undertake compliance assistance activities. The added support of our partners enhances the scope and effect of both enforcement and compliance assistance. WHD's national partnership activities include (but are certainly not limited to) collaboration with the following organizations.

Federal Network for Young Worker Safety and Health (FedNet)

The Department is a founding member of FedNet, a partnership of 14 federal agencies that share ideas, resources, and opportunities to keep young workers safe. This program strives to:

- Increase awareness of young worker occupational safety and health among key community players and young workers as they enter the workforce;
- Foster education, training, and outreach to promote young worker safety and health;
- Enhance federal initiatives that create relationships with small businesses, trade associations, and other organizations that employ young workers; and
- Promote resources that enhance employer compliance and knowledge of federal and state regulations related to young workers.

FedNet accomplishments include safe summer job kick-offs, brochures, and safety tips. The collaboration available through FedNet enhances opportunities for WHD to disseminate materials and information.

National Institute for Occupational Safety and Health (NIOSH) and the Occupational Safety and Health Administration (OSHA)

WHD has a longstanding partnership with NIOSH in the areas of improving workplace safety for young workers and in the collection and interpretation of injury and fatality data, especially as it related to rulemaking efforts. In 1998, WHD provided funding to NIOSH to conduct a comprehensive review of scientific literature and available data in order to assess current workplace hazards and the adequacy of the current child labor HOs. The report, entitled *National Institute for Occupational Safety and Health (NIOSH) Recommendations to the U.S. Department of Labor for Changes to Hazardous Orders* (NIOSH report), was issued in July 2002. The NIOSH report, which makes 35 recommendations concerning the existing non-agricultural HOs and recommends the creation of 17 new HOs, was the impetus for the Department's April 2007 Notice of Proposed Rulemaking (NPRM).

In addition, WHD and OSHA have, for many years, been active members of the NIOSH-sponsored *Federal Interagency Work Group on Preventing Childhood Agricultural Injury.* This group, whose membership includes representatives of the U.S. Department of Agriculture (USDA), works to reduce young farm-worker deaths and injuries.

Finally, WHD works with NIOSH and OSHA in a "rapid response" young worker fatality notification system that keeps all three agencies advised of youth workplace deaths.

Young Workers Health and Safety Network (YWN)

WHD has also worked for many years with the YWN, a subcommittee of the Occupational Health and Safety Section of the American Public Health Association, to promote compliance with the child labor provisions and to reduce occupational injuries to and workplace deaths of minors. The YWN—which describes itself as an informal network of public health professionals, advocates, and government agency staff— includes individuals from academia, public health, labor law enforcement, health and safety consultation and enforcement, and labor organizations.

Interstate Labor Standards Association (ILSA)

WHD has an active collaborative relationship with ILSA, an organization of state labor department officials. As part of this ongoing coordination, WHD officials at the national, regional, and local organizations levels communicate with State labor departments on various child labor activities.

U. S. Department of Agriculture (USDA)

Given the higher fatality rates among young workers in the agricultural industry, WHD works with USDA on many issues. WHD's most recent collaboration with USDA involves the reinvention and streamlining of the tractor certification program. Under the child labor agricultural HOs, 14- and 15-year-olds may operate certain otherwise prohibited farm equipment after being properly trained and certified in the safe operation of the equipment. In most cases, agricultural extension service agents or agricultural vocational school instructors perform the training, testing, and certification based on requirements established by regulation. These requirements have become outdated, many of the training materials are no longer in print, and because of funding reallocations, not all states now provide the training or certification. The interagency agricultural HO Steering Committee has overseen the identification of the required skill sets, the development of a modern curriculum with multiple methods of delivery, the engineering of an electronic system that will register teachers, administer examinations, issue certificates, and monitor the operation of the entire process. WHD continues to work with USDA to ensure the completion of this important project.

Equal Employment Opportunity Commission (EEOC)

WHD works with EEOC to ensure that young workers experience a workplace free from discrimination and sexual harassment. WHD and EEOC jointly provide compliance assistance to employers of workers with disabilities—many of whom are under the age of 18.

National Children's Center for Rural and Agricultural Health and Safety (NCCRAHS)

NCCRAHS, based in Marshfield, Wisconsin, strives to enhance the health and safety of all children exposed to hazards associated with agricultural work and rural environments. NCCRAHS receives funding from NIOSH. WHD staff have served on the NCCRAHS steering committee and have helped develop and disseminate the North American Guidelines for Children's Agricultural Tasks (NAGCAT). NAGCAT is a collection of guidelines designed to assist parents and others in assigning age-appropriate tasks for children ages 7 to 16 that live or work on farms and ranches across North America. The guidelines are based on an understanding of childhood growth and development, agricultural practices, principles of childhood injury, and agricultural and occupational safety. Voluntary use of the guidelines can help parents and others make informed decisions about appropriate tasks for youth.

Regulatory and Legislative Initiatives Have Strengthened Child Labor Laws

Because of changes in the workplace, the introduction of new processes and technologies, the emergence of new types of businesses in which young workers may find employment opportunities, the existence of differing federal and state standards, and divergent views on how best to balance scholastic requirements and work experiences, the Department has for many years been conducting an ongoing review of the criteria for permissible child labor employment. Some of the most significant accomplishments towards protecting working young men and women in this country are reflected in the recent revisions to the child labor regulations.

On December 16, 2004, the Department published a final rule that amended the child labor regulations to implement statutory amendments to two existing HOs: the Compactors and Balers Safety Standards Modernization Act, affecting paper balers and compactors (HO No. 12); and the Teen Drive for Employment Act, affecting teenagers whose jobs may include driving on public roads (HO 2). The regulations also updated the types of cooking activities allowed for 14- and 15-year-olds; revised the "roofing" HO to ban all work on or about roofs by youths under age 18; updated the definition of "explosives" in HO 1; and reduced paperwork in processing age certificates.

As previously noted, the NIOSH report made recommendations concerning the existing non-agricultural HOs and recommended the creation of 17 new HOs. Upon receiving the NIOSH report, WHD conducted a detailed review and met with various stakeholders to evaluate and prioritize each recommendation for possible regulatory action consistent with the established national policy of balancing the benefits of employment opportunities for youth with the necessary and appropriate safety protections. The 2004 final rule addressed six of the NIOSH recommendations.

In April 2007, the Department published an NPRM and an Advance Notice of Proposed Rulemaking (ANPRM) as part of its continuing efforts to update the youth employment regulations for the 21st Century. The current proposals would represent the most significant revisions to the child labor regulations in 30 years. The proposals would strengthen youth employment regulations to protect against workplace hazards, expand youth workplace opportunities that have been judged safe and permissible, update regulations to better reflect the modern workplace, and address many of the remaining recommendations from the NIOSH report. WHD is in the process of drafting a final rule based on the comments it received in response to the NPRM, and anticipates transmitting that rule to the Office of Management and Budget shortly. WHD continues to review the comments received in response to the ANPRM, and the remaining NIOSH recommendations, for potential future rulemaking.

For the last several years, the President's budget has included a legislative proposal to increase the amount of civil money penalties that could be assessed for child labor violations that cause the serious injury or death of a young worker. On May 21 of this year, President Bush signed into law the Genetic Information Nondiscrimination Act of 2008 (GINA). Among other things, GINA amends the FLSA by increasing the civil money penalties that may be imposed for child labor violations resulting in death or serious injury. The legislation raised the maximum penalty to $50,000 for each violation resulting in the death of or serious injury to working youth. In cases where the employer's violation is repeated or willful, the maximum penalty was raised to $100,000. This new authority provides WHD with an important tool in securing compliance with the child labor provisions.

IMPROVEMENTS IN CHILD LABOR COMPLIANCE—A CONTINUING PRIORITY FOR WHD

As we have demonstrated, ensuring that young workers in this country have safe and appropriate early work experiences has been and continues to be a high priority for this agency. It is an integral part of every investigation, and WHD personnel nationwide are committed to this agency goal. WHD has used and continues to use every tool available—enforcement, compliance assistance, public awareness, partnership, regulation, and legislation—to promote compliance with the Nation's child labor laws. We believe that we have demonstrated success in these efforts, but as in every program, we look for opportunities to improve. Last year, the Department began working with an independent evaluator to assess our strategies and their effectiveness in increasing compliance with the FLSA child labor provisions. That study is ongoing, and we look forward to any recommended opportunities for improvements that may come. In examining our activities and accomplishments, however, we can cite several measures of success.

WHD has conducted two national, statistically valid, investigation-based compliance surveys of youth employed in the grocery store and restaurant industries. These are two industries that employ a high percentage of young workers. The first baseline survey was conducted in 2000 to gauge the level of child labor compliance in full-service restaurants, quick-service restaurants, and grocery stores. A second investigation-based survey was conducted in 2004 to determine if the levels of compliance had changed. These two surveys were full on-site investigations that not only included interviews of the young workers, but also included interviews with their coworkers and employers. The investigation-based surveys allowed WHD investigators to establish coverage under the FLSA, review payroll records, and make conclusive determinations on whether the teens were employed in violation of applicable federal law.

The 2004 investigation-based survey showed continued high levels of child labor compliance in the full-service restaurant and grocery store industries, similar to the levels found in 2000. The 2004 survey also demonstrated improvements in child labor compliance in quick-service restaurants in comparison to the 2000 survey results. WHD found significant reductions in the percentage of employers with repeat violations in all three industries. The 2004 survey investigations found that 91 percent of quick-service restaurants were in compliance with the FLSA child labor provisions and that 99 percent of youth employed in this industry were employed in compliance. The survey also found 73 percent of full-service restaurants were in compliance and 88 percent of youth workers were employed in compliance. Finally, 80 percent of grocery stores were in compliance and 95 percent of youth were employed in compliance in this industry. Ninety-six (96) percent of full- and quick-service restaurants and 88 percent of grocery stores were in compliance with the child labor HO provisions. The high percentage of youth employed in compliance and the increase in compliance among prior violators can be attributed to the compliance activities of the agency during the intervening year between the surveys. Those efforts continue today.

The 2004 survey results are not the only indicators of improved compliance. In FY 2007, WHD completed an investigation-based compliance survey, *i.e.*, the Youth Employment Survey (YES), to determine child labor compliance in four large national retail chains, Sears, Roebuck and Company (Sears); K-Mart; Wal-Mart Stores, Inc. (Wal- Mart); and Target Corporation (Target). All four companies had a history of child labor violations. Following the prior investigations, Sears and Wal-Mart had entered into settlement agreements with WHD to promote future child labor compliance.

Of the 67 establishments investigated, WHD found 82 percent (55 of 67) in full compliance with the child labor provisions. All establishments, but one, were in compliance with the child labor hours standards. Eight-four (84) percent of the establishments were in compliance with the child labor HOs. In total, 40 child labor violations were found involving 36 minors; one child labor hours violation and 39 HO violations. Of the 39 HO violations cited, 38 involved violations of HO No. 12 (balers). One HO No. 7 (forklift) violation was found. The findings in this initiative contributed, in part, to WHD’s decision to place an emphasis on increasing compliance with HO No. 12 as part of its fiscal year 2008 performance plan.

Sears was fully in compliance, with no child labor violations found. One Wal-Mart establishment was found in violation with a single HO No. 12 violation. Three Target establishments accounted for 14 violations involving 11 minors. K-Mart has the highest rate of non-compliance, with 7 stores having 24 violations involving 23 minors. These large corporate enterprises, that employ minors nationwide, have far fewer child labor violations and are far more aware of their obligations as a result of WHD's continued presence.

While these measures of compliance are encouraging, the declines in workplace injuries and fatalities are the most significant indicators of improved working conditions for young workers in this country. According to NIOSH-provided statistics, 38 youth under the age of 18 died from work-related injuries in 2007—a significant drop from the average of 61 youth aged

17 and under who were killed on the job during the years 1998 to 2002. Equally encouraging is the corresponding decline in youth fatality rates from a high of more than 3.5 per 100,000 FTE in 1999 to approximately 2 per 100,000 FTE in 2006. Injuries to young workers have also declined in recent years, although not as sharply as fatalities. In 1999, NIOSH estimated that over 70,000 14-to 17-year-olds were injured on the job seriously enough to warrant a trip to a hospital emergency room. By 2006, the estimate had dropped to 52,600.

The agency believes these injury and fatality results demonstrate significant progress in addressing child labor violations. The actions and activities of many parties have contributed to these declining statistics, but clearly too many minors continue to be injured while working, and even one death of a working teen is one too many. The challenge of protecting the welfare of young workers is a shared responsibility. It rests with federal and state officials, parents, educators, community-based and advocacy organizations, employers, and the young workers themselves. WHD remains committed to this challenge and will continue to promote legal employment opportunities for young men and women that are safe, positive, and do not distract from or interfere with their education.

Thank you again for this opportunity to discuss this important issue. This concludes my prepared statement. I would be glad to answer any questions.

In: Child Labor in America
Ed: I. C. Rivera and N. M. Howard
ISBN: 978-1-60876-769-4

Chapter 4

CHILD LABOR ENFORCEMENT HEARING: TESTIMONY OF DAVID A. STRAUSS

David A. Strauss
Association of Farmworker Opportunity Programs

Representative Woolsey and members of the subcommittee, thank you for inviting me to testify this morning on the conditions endured by children who work for wages in the farms, fields and orchards of America. I also want to comment on the lack of enforcement of child labor laws in the agriculture industry and recommend changes to the law that will give the same protections to children working in agricultures as other children enjoy.

The Association of Farmworker Opportunity Programs is the national federation of nonprofit and public agencies that conduct job training programs for eligible migrant and seasonal farmworkers throughout the United States. In the mid-1990s, our members noticed that in many places young children were preparing and harvesting crops, often but not always alongside their parents or other family members. As they began looking into this, they realized that the Fair Labor Standards Act (FLSA) actually permits children as young as 12 and in rare instances as young as 10 to work in agriculture. I'm not talking about family farms, where sons and daughters of farmers learn the business firsthand at a young age. I'm talking about working farms that employ large numbers of workers who aren't related to the owners.

There are about 2.5 million people who earn their living, at least in part, by performing farmwork in this country. Among them, tens of thousands migrate among various states each year, following the crops and seeking work wherever they can find it. Often, families are traveling from Texas or Florida to the upper Midwest, Southeast and Northeast. In California, there are many workers that migrate long distances often within that state. They are typically paid miserably low wages, receive no job-related benefits, and have no job security. The average farmworker family earns less than $15,000 per year from all sources, well below the federal poverty level. In this situation, they sometimes require their children to work to help bring in more income. While there are no reliable statistics on children that work in the fields, our research indicates that there are about 400,000 such young people below the age of 18.

The FLSA requires that they not work during school hours when school is in session. That is virtually the only restriction in federal law, along with a prohibition against hazardous employment for children 15 and younger. That means that a 12 year old kid can work 12 or more hours a day during the summer, on weekends, or during the school year as long as those hours are outside of school time. I have spoken with teenage children of migrant families who worked after school until midnight during a heavy harvest.

That same child, if he worked in my office, could only work at most three hours during a school day after school is out, and no more than 40 hours a week in the summer. And my offices are air conditioned and comfortable. The fields are not. One of my staff completed a two week visit to North Carolina's blueberry fields this past June and found dozens of kids, some as young as 6, working in 105 degree heat all day long for several weeks at a time. California, for example, has heat illness prevention standards to protect child workers, but the Federal Secretary of Labor has not issued a Hazardous Occupation Order for excessive heat.

The toll on the children is real. Sometimes their families take them out of school before the end of the semester, and return after the new school year begins. While in many places there are federally funded migrant education programs available, those programs aren't always congruent with those in the home state school, so children lose the credits they thought they were earning. They start the year behind, and have to work doubly hard to catch up, even while they may be working in fields again after school. Their parents typically do not have much formal education and may speak English very poorly, so they aren't in the same environment of learning as most of their peers, nor can their parents afford tutors or other special aids.

The results are predictable: most migrant children, perhaps more than 67%, drop out of school well before high school graduation. Without a diploma, without good job skills, they often end up continuing the cycle of poverty their parents hoped they could break. It is a tragic waste that we cannot allow to continue. Most of these children want to succeed, know the meaning and value of hard work, but are cut off from accessing the American Dream as soon as they drop out.

While in my opinion, the law is not sufficiently protective of child agricultural workers, my staff has observed violation after violation of FLSA provisions. For example, one staff member saw children below the age of twelve working for pay with no sign of any inspector. The law was broken in 11 of the 12 farms she visited; where were the wage and hour people? This needs to stop. The federal government and the states need to make a renewed commitment to protecting our youngest workers.

In addition, Congress should equalize the protections of these children with the rest of America's workforce. Amend the FLSA to protect children working in agriculture just the same as we protect children working in nearly every other industry. Representative Lucille Roybal-Allard introduced a bill (HR 2674) in June 2007 that would do just that. Finally, we must dramatically increase the federal commitment to the development of farmworker children. Legal protections alone won't assure their progress, so we have to invest in those actions we know will keep them in school and allow them to become as successful as Norma has.

The reality is that under our very noses, this country has a farm labor sector that resembles similar sectors in third world countries. It is a disgrace that the people who prepare and harvest our food often barely earn enough to purchase the food that their families need to survive. The least we can do is protect their children and give them a chance at the American Dream.

Thank you for your time and attention and I'll be glad to answer any questions you might have.

In: Child Labor in America
Ed: I. C. Rivera and N. M. Howard
ISBN: 978-1-60876-769-4

Chapter 5

CHILD LABOR ENFORCEMENT: ARE WE ADEQUATELY PROTECTING OUR CHILDREN?

Lynn Woolsey
Subcommittee on Workforce Protections

WASHINGTON, D.C. – *Below are the prepared remarks of U.S. Rep. Lynn Woolsey (D-CA), chairwoman of the Subcommittee on Workforce Protections, for a subcommittee hearing on "Child Labor Enforcement: Are We Adequately Protecting Our Children?"*

I want to welcome you all today for a hearing on "Child Labor Enforcement: Are We Adequately Protecting Our Children?"

While we will primarily examine the current state of enforcement of our federal child labor laws by the Department of Labor, I hope that our witnesses will also address how the Fair Labor Standards Act (FLSA) treats children who work in agriculture differently than those who work in other industries.

The fact is that children who work on a farm are allowed to work at a younger age, for longer hours and in more hazardous conditions than kids who work at a grocery store.

This is unacceptable.

This difference is a throwback to another era when one-quarter of Americans still lived on family farms and a majority of the agricultural work performed by children was done on behalf of their family.

While times have changed and less than 2% of Americans live on farms today, our laws have not.

As a result of technical advances and the growth of large-scale agriculture, most children working in the fields are hired as laborers on large commercial farms. This is a far cry from the family farm.

Representative Roybal-Allard's CARE Act, would correct this imbalance by raising protections for child farm workers to the same level of children working in other industries.

I am proud to be a cosponsor of this legislation, which we will give serious attention to next year.

Representative Bruce Braley has just introduced a bill to increase criminal sanctions on employers who exploit children.

Last year I introduced a bi-partisan bill, the Child Care Protection Act, which increases penalties and establishes a ($50,000) civil penalty for a violation which causes the death or serious injury of a child laborer.

And my good friend, Ranking Member Wilson is an original co-sponsor of the bill.

The provisions of the bill were signed into law this year as part of the Genetic Information Non- Discrimination Act.

This is progress.

However, as I said when the child labor penalty bill was passed, this is a first good step, but additional enforcement measures are needed to adequately protect our children.

Unfortunately, all the legislation in the world won't help if we are not able to adequately enforce our child labor laws.

And it is clear that this Administration does not appear to be focused on enforcing the laws already on the books.

Let me give you a few examples:

The Wage and Hour Division has 730 inspectors for the entire country, down from 945 in 2001.

These inspectors are charged with enforcing all aspects of the FLSA, which in addition to child labor, include minimum wage and overtime protections.

And it appears from the numbers that the Wage and Hour Division spends little time investigating child labor complaints as opposed to other violations.

In 2005, for example, the Division devoted less than 5 percent of its total investigatory time on child labor matters.

And only a small fraction of this time is devoted to investigations in the agricultural sector.

In FY2007, the DOL uncovered 4,672 children who were working in violation of federal child safety laws.

Four years earlier, DOL found double that number.

I find it hard to believe that child labor violations have decreased by half over that time period.

There are serious violations of child labor laws that need DOL's attention.

For example, on September 9, the State of Iowa filed over 9,000 counts of state child labor law violations at Agriprocessors, a meatpacking plant in Postville, Iowa.

You are all undoubtedly familiar with Agriprocessors, which was the site of the one of the largest workplace immigration raids in U.S. history.

The State alleges that 32 children, seven of whom were under the age of 16, were employed at the plant in violation of the prohibition against children working in meatpacking facilities.

In addition, these children were exposed to dangerous chemicals, and children under 16 were found to be illegally operating power machinery, working during prohibited hours, and in excess of the hours allowed by law.

These allegations also appear to be violations of federal law, but while the Immigration and Customs Enforcement (ICE) was out in droves, DOL has been missing in action.

It is hard to claim adequate enforcement with that kind of a record, but I look forward to hearing from Mr. Passantino and our other witness on this issue.

With that, I defer to the ranking member, Joe Wilson, for his opening statement.

http://edlabor.house.gov

In: Child Labor in America
Ed: I. C. Rivera and N. M. Howard
ISBN: 978-1-60876-769-4

Chapter 6

CHILD LABOR IN AMERICA: HISTORY, POLICY, AND LEGISLATIVE ISSUES*

Gerald Mayer
Labor Policy Domestic Social Policy Division

SUMMARY

The history of child labor in America is long and, in some cases, unsavory. It dates back to the founding of the United States. Traditionally, most children, except for the privileged few, had always worked — either for their parents or for an outside employer. Through the years, however, child labor practices have changed. So have the benefits and risks associated with employment of children. In some respects, altered workplace technology has served to make work easier and less hazardous. At the same time, some processes and equipment have rendered the workplace more dangerous, especially for children and youth.

Child labor first became a federal legislative issue at least as far back as 1906 with the introduction of the Beveridge proposal for regulation of the types of work in which children might be engaged. Although the 1906 legislation was not adopted, it led to extended study of the conditions under which children were employed or allowed to work and to a series of legislative

* This is an edited, reformatted and augmented version of a CRS Report for Congress publication dated October 2008.

proposals — some approved, others defeated or overturned by the courts — culminating in the Fair Labor Standards Act (FLSA) of 1938. The latter statute, amended periodically, remains the primary federal law dealing with the employment of children.

Although providing a framework for regulation of child labor (and, in some cases, forbidding it entirely), the FLSA is not comprehensive, nor does it deal with all employment of children in precisely the same way. Generally speaking, work by young persons (under 18 years of age) in mines and factories is not allowed. The types of nonfarm work that may be suitable (or especially hazardous) for persons under 18 years of age has been left mainly to the discretion of the Secretary of Labor. Some types of work — for example, some newspaper sales and delivery, theatrical (and related) employment — fall beyond the scope of FLSA child labor requirements. Finally, a distinction has been made between employment in nonagricultural fields and in agriculture and, in the latter case, between work for a parent or guardian in an agricultural setting and commercial employment.

In the 110th Congress, a range of child labor legislation has been introduced. Legislation was enacted that imposes greater civil penalties on employers who violate the child labor provisions of the FLSA.

This report examines, briefly, the historical issue of child labor in America. It looks at various bills that have been introduced in the 108th, 109th, and 110th Congresses. It will be updated as developments warrant.

Efforts to regulate (or to prohibit) certain forms of child labor in America largely commenced late in the 19th century, mostly at the state level.[1] During the first decade of the 20th century, child labor became a federal concern. Congressional hearings were followed by extensive study of the issue — and by several unsuccessful efforts to deal with child labor through law. Finally, with the adoption of the Fair Labor Standards Act (FLSA) of 1938, the modern federal role in child labor regulation took shape. But, debate concerning the issue has continued in Congress.[2]

Through the years, regulation of child labor has been contentious, sparking sharp differences of opinion. Some have urged modification of existing federal child labor restraints to afford greater opportunities for young persons to learn the value of work or to gain entry into a skilled occupation. But, the opportunity to learn a craft and industrial discipline can also provide an occasion for youth to be exploited and, possibly, endangered. Some have questioned whether young children ought to be employed at all, especially while attending school.

Discussion of child labor would seem to suggest trade-offs, resting upon fundamental socioeconomic philosophy and the value one places upon time. For example, when is child labor a healthy and useful introduction to the world-of-work? And, when might it divert young persons from academic work or place them at physical (or psychological) risk? Do children (however defined) need time for their own purposes and, if so, how much time? How might one distinguish between freedom (to play, think, or associate informally with peers) and idleness that may be conducive to activities that may be less wholesome than some types of work? Is some work suitable for young children and teenagers (persons less than 18 years of age) and, if so, how might suitable work be distinguished from work that is not suitable or that is "particularly hazardous" for persons of that age?

The history of child labor in American workplaces can be divided, roughly, into four periods. First, from the late 19th century to 1941, reformers sought to remove children from the workplace (whether factory, field, or tenement house) and to encourage more extended school attendance. Second, with World War II, the focus shifted to alleged labor shortages for war production. Some urged modification of work restrictions for older children: too young for the draft but old enough to be useful employees. Third, by the late 1940s, another shift took place. Too many older youths were believed to be out of school, out of work, and unable to find employment for which, it was argued, they were often unprepared both in terms of training and discipline. Thus, various "school-to-work" transition programs were developed together with "incentives" for employers to hire youth workers. Fourth, since roughly the late 1980s, child labor in its various aspects has largely disappeared from the policy scene; the issue is often viewed as a remnant of an earlier and darker period in American history.

This report is intended as an introduction to the issue of child labor. It briefly describes the early history of child labor regulation, reviews recent federal initiatives in that area, and discusses concerns voiced through the 110th Congress.

EARLY CHILD LABOR IN AMERICA

Prior to the 20th century, employment of children largely reflected socioeconomic class stratification. Where children were of working-class families, it was largely assumed that they would work — even when they were very young. Some were employed in the street trades: delivering newspapers and telegrams, shining boots and shoes, running errands in various (often, unwholesome) sections of the city, and at whatever hours the task demanded. Others were engaged in industrial homework: in tasks often reserved for the very young who could work, usually alongside a parent or another adult, in a tenement flat in segments of garment production or in other types of work that could be performed, sometimes on a piece rate basis, in one's place of residence. Still others worked in mines or factories: most notoriously, perhaps, the "breaker boys" (who separated coal from slate and rock) in the coal mines, the child workers in the textile mills, and the helpers in the glass factories.

Agricultural labor by children seems always to have been in a category by itself. Usually, until the early 20th century, such work seems to have been on the family farm (whatever its size) or in an agricultural operation in the general vicinity of a youth's place of residence, though he (or she) might reside and work beyond the view and reach of a parent. Such work was no less hazardous — and no less arduous — than that of the streets or tenement or industrial labor. Indeed, in some respects, agricultural work may have been more dangerous.

Regulation of child labor has been motivated by diverse concerns: economic, humane, and more broadly social. In the 19th and early 20th centuries, child workers were often viewed as an alternative source of low-wage labor who vied with their parents and other adults for employment — even at the cost of their own health and education. Products of child labor competed with goods produced by adults, exerting a downward pressure on wages and living standards. Aside from health and safety hazards, inadequate rest, it was argued, left children ill-suited for educational activities and, in turn, as adults, ill-prepared for employment or for the support of their own children, thus extending the cycle of poverty and adding to social-welfare costs.[3]

Opposition to Child Labor Begins to Organize

The trade union movement early voiced strong opposition to child labor. New York labor activist Samuel Gompers championed child labor reform during the late 19th century and later, as president of the American Federation of Labor (AFL), used his influence to improve the lot of working children.[4] Worker's advocate "Mother" (Mary Harris) Jones brought added visibility to the plight of child workers and to that of their parents as well.[5] After its organization in 1899, the National Consumers League (NCL), under the leadership of Florence Kelley, took up the campaign against child labor as did a significant body of social workers, clergy, and concerned individuals.[6] In 1904, these forces were drawn together with the establishment of the National Child Labor Committee (NCLC) which, thereafter, would remain a central force in the movement to end exploitation of children in the workplace.[7]

Child labor regulation generally commenced at the state level. Early laws were experimental, loosely drawn, and, where they exerted a restraining influence, subject to court challenge. Each type of work by children — for example, in the mines, factories, fields, or street trades — presented its own special challenges for reformers; but, industrial homework by children was especially difficult to restrain. Although often not formally employed, children worked in tenement sweatshops making clothing, processing food, and engaging in whatever other work might profitably be conducted at home. Any tenement might become a little factory where conditions were adverse (often, effectively unregulated) and hours of work were unrestrained except by exhaustion. Thus, child labor and industrial homework, from a regulatory/reform perspective, became intermeshed. Reformers tended to agree that child labor could not be controlled while industrial homework continued: that regulation of the latter, per se, would never be successful. A total ban on the system, they said, was needed.[8]

Reformers, however, did not always agree on timing or overall strategy. Most seem to have concurred that, ultimately, reform would need to be federal. Faced with state regulation of child labor or industrial homework, employers could simply move to another state. Further, those who utilized child labor could play one jurisdiction against another in terms of wage-based economic development. For labor standards, it was a race to the bottom. At the same time, the strength of reform organization varied from one state to another. Some believed that state action was more nearly feasible than securing broader national change, at least at that time.

The Early Federal Role in Child Labor Regulation

In 1906, Senator Albert Beveridge (R-IN) and Representative Herbert Parsons (R-NY) introduced legislation to prevent employment of children in factories and mines. Debate on this first federal initiative continued through several years but it did not become law. However, with the work of the various reform groups, the proposal raised the visibility of child labor as a public policy issue.[9] In 1907, legislation was approved (P.L. 59-41) which authorized the Secretary of Commerce and Labor (then, a single department) "to investigate and report upon the industrial, social, moral, education[al], and physical condition of woman and child workers in the United States." The result was a detailed survey which appeared in 19 volumes between 1910 and 1913.[10] Building from that evidentiary record, Congress turned again to the legislative process to deal with child labor and related problems.

The Child Labor Initiatives (1916-1924)

Although Congress and the advocates of reform sought to limit exploitive/oppressive child labor, the best approach was not immediately clear. Thus, sequentially, Congress moved in three directions — each uniformly unsuccessful.

In 1916, a decade after the Beveridge proposal, new federal child labor legislation was introduced by Senator Robert Owen (D-OK) and by Representative Edward Keating (D-CO) with support from the reform community. A regional struggle then in progress pitted one state against another in a contest for economic growth with low-wage nonunion labor a bargaining chip. Southern manufacturers viewed child labor restriction as an "effort of northern agitators to kill the infant industries of the south."[11] The Owen-Keating Act (1916), based on the commerce clause of the Constitution, sought to ban movement in interstate commerce of certain products of child labor. In June 1918, however, the Supreme Court declared the act unconstitutional (*Hammer v. Dagenhart*, 247 U.S. 251), and reformers searched for a new approach.[12]

Congress next turned to the taxing power as an indirect method for controlling child labor. Senator Atlee Pomerene (D-OH) proposed to levy a 10% tax "on the annual net profits of industries" that employed children in violation of certain age and hours standards.[13] The tax penalty would offset any competitive advantage that child labor might otherwise provide. Although the measure was in reality child labor legislation, it was hoped that it might secure Court approval. The Supreme Court demurred and the Pomerene (child labor tax) Act (1919) was declared unconstitutional in May 1922 (*Bailey v. Drexel Furniture Company*, 259 U.S. 20).[14]

In the wake of the *Drexel* case, Samuel Gompers met at AFL headquarters with Florence Kelley of the National Consumers League, representatives of the NCLC, and others. After extended discussion and a weighing of options, the group developed a proposal for a constitutional amendment to grant Congress the right "to limit, regulate, and prohibit the labor of persons under 18 years of age." The child labor amendment (1924) involved far more than the mere passing of legislation since the case for approval had to be made to each state legislature. While the proponents of child labor reform began optimistically, support began to erode on a number of fronts for reasons not necessarily associated with child labor per se. The proposed amendment remained unratified in 1937 when Congress turned back to direct legislation with consideration of the Fair Labor Standards Act.[15]

Early New Deal Enactments (1933-1937)

From the period of the Beveridge bill (1906) to the New Deal era, children's advocates remained divided over the means for ending exploitive child labor. The reform community initially split with respect to federal action. Then, it had largely coalesced behind the Owen- Keating (1916) and Pomerene (1918) bills, debating long and hard over the wisdom of a constitutional amendment (1924). By late 1932, leaders of the Children's Bureau in the Department of Labor (DOL) and the NCLC, with others, decided to shift their focus away from ratification of the constitutional amendment (which was then perceived to be in doubt) and back toward action by individual states.

In retrospect, this shift of emphasis may have been a misreading of the times. "By 1933," notes Walter Trattner in his reform-oriented study, *Crusade for the Children*, "the spreading contagion of child labor had found every weakness and loophole in state labor legislation." He observes: "Sweatshops and fly-by-night plants were exploiting children for little or no pay, moving at will across state lines to take advantage of laws of nearby states. The individual states were unable to halt these abuses which had far-reaching effects, including the complete breakdown of wage scales." Thus, in competitive terms, some argued, it was not feasible for individual states to lead in labor-related reform, even were they predisposed to do so. Trattner concludes: "Everywhere people were looking to Washington for help and direction."[16]

Soon after the inauguration of President Franklin D. Roosevelt, Congress passed the National Industrial Recovery Act (NIRA, 1933). Under the National Recovery Administration (NRA), industries were encouraged to develop codes of fair competition, which in many instances came to include minimum wage and overtime pay standards, a ban on industrial homework, and the restriction or elimination of child labor. Elimination of child labor under the Cotton Textile Code seemed, momentarily, a major breakthrough. However, in May 1935, the NIRA was declared unconstitutional (*Schechter Poultry Corp. et al v. United States*, 295 U.S. 495).[17]

The Agricultural Adjustment Act (AAA) of May 1933 and the Jones-Costigan Sugar Stabilization Act (1934) were roughly companion measures to the NIRA. In exchange for certain price supports, the government required grower/producer adherence to certain labor and marketing standards.[18] In 1937, the AAA was similarly declared unconstitutional.

In an effort to salvage NIRA and AAA labor standards, less comprehensive measures followed. First, Labor Secretary Frances Perkins, long a child labor reformer, urged that government, as a consumer (a more likely constitutional strategy), refuse to purchase items produced by child labor or under unsafe and unclean conditions in tenements (industrial homework). These restrictions were made part of the Public Contracts Act (1936), co-sponsored by Senator David Walsh (D-MA) and Representative Arthur Healey (D-MA), also called the Walsh-Healey Act.[19] Second. Agricultural labor standards, though limited, reemerged in the Beet Sugar Act (1937), again linked to a federal support system.[20]

The FLSA and General Child Labor Regulation (1938).

Following adoption of Walsh-Healey, Secretary Perkins urged passage of general federal minimum wage and overtime pay legislation. Trattner notes that Roosevelt, possibly believing that the wage/hour measure could more easily be enacted "if it were made more attractive by integrating it with child labor," combined the several provisions.[21] Perkins recalls that child labor provisions were added, late in the process, at the urging of Grace Abbott, for many years head of the Children's Bureau at DOL. "The President readily agreed and was delighted that we might make this bill cover child labor as well as low wages and long hours."[22] After exhaustive debate, the Fair Labor Standards Act (FLSA), with its child labor provisions, became law during the summer of 1938.[23]

The FLSA was not a complete victory for advocates of child labor regulation. Historian Jeremy Felt argues that the act may have served "as a deterrent and as an educational force" but adds that "in those areas where children are useful they continue to be employed."[24] Further, the act did not deal with competition from goods produced abroad by child workers under conditions the FLSA proscribed in America.

During the early 1940s, as enforcement of the FLSA commenced, DOL found (like reformers early in the century) that illegal exploitation of children as laborers was extremely difficult to eradicate where industrial homework persisted. Attempts to regulate the latter were largely unproductive. By the mid-1940s, DOL had imposed an outright ban on industrial homework in certain garment-related fields. Thereafter, abusive child labor seems to have faded as a public policy issue, gradually being replaced by concern with youth unemployment, training, and "school-to-work" transition.[25]

CHILD LABOR UNDER THE FAIR LABOR STANDARDS ACT

The FLSA, as amended, protects children by setting conditions under which they may be employed and, in certain types of work, prohibiting their employment altogether.[26] Although the basic structure of the act has changed little since 1938, Congress has altered specific provisions of the statute and DOL has variously refined its administration through the rulemaking process.

The Basic Pattern of Coverage

Under the FLSA, employers may not use "oppressive child labor in commerce or in the production of goods for commerce." "Oppressive" is partially defined in the act and partly left to the discretion of the Secretary. Persons under 18 years of age may not be employed in mining or manufacturing or "in any occupation which the Secretary of Labor shall ... declare to be particularly hazardous for the employment of children ... or detrimental to their health or well-being." Otherwise, 16 years of age is the usual minimum age for employment. The Secretary may permit employment of persons 14 to 16 years of age in work not deemed "oppressive," that does not interfere with the youth's schooling, and that is not detrimental to his/her "health and well-being." The Secretary has established hours during which children of various ages may work: that is, the number of hours they may be employed, taking into account the demands of academic attendance.

Exemptions

The Fair Labor Standards Act is a broad umbrella statute that sets forth general policies and, at the same time, may specify in precise detail, either in the statute per se or through implementing regulations, how coverage is to be applied: namely, who is covered and who is exempt. Because of the technical nature of wage/hour and child labor law, it may be unwise to accept any segment of the statute (or regulations) in isolation and at face value. Most provisions of the act have either been the subject of litigation or have long administrative/legislative histories. What may seem obvious on the surface may, in fact, be inordinately complex.[27]

The FLSA, rooted in the commerce clause of the Constitution, excludes from coverage children who are not involved in activities affecting interstate commerce — though such persons may be protected by state statutes. Also excluded are children employed by "a parent or a person standing in place of a parent employing his own child or a child in his custody." A child, for instance, assisting a parent (helping around a "mom-and-pop" corner grocery or doing chores around the home) would not be covered under federal child labor law. Nor do the child labor provisions of the act apply to children employed as actors or in related activities. Traditionally, the "street trades" (such as newspaper delivery) have been regarded as appropriate for children and, thus, are not restrained by FLSA child labor provisions. During the mid-1990s, the Departmental regulations were altered, administratively, to allow youths of 14 and 15 years of age to work in certain "sports-attending services at professional sporting events."

Child/youth employment in agriculture is treated somewhat differently from nonagricultural employment.[28] For example, a child working for a parent on a family farm is not covered under the FLSA. The law and regulations include differences with respect to age and the types of work that children and teenagers may perform. (See **Table 1** for a general summary of these requirements.) Under the 1977 amendments to the act, a specialized exemption, carefully circumscribed, was written into the statute for the employment of children of 10 and 11 years of age as hand harvest workers in agriculture.[29]

Enforcement

Even where child labor is banned, enforcement can be difficult. FLSA compliance staff is relatively small, and enforcement is often complaint driven. Child workers, themselves, may not be likely to complain. If children are employed with parental knowledge or consent, complaints from their family may not be frequent — even where such employment may be illegal or hazardous to the child. Where migratory agricultural work is concerned, enforcement problems are more complex.

Children, like adults, work for diverse reasons: to have spending money or to save for their education or other reasons. But, they may also enter the workforce under pressure from parents who believe that employment, even for young children, provides good discipline and keeps youngsters off the street and out of mischief. A traditional argument for child labor has been economic necessity: that is, contributing to family income. If child workers and their parents fail to cooperate in the enforcement of child labor law, then DOL compliance activity can become extremely difficult.

Table 1. Summary of Child Labor Regulation Under the Fair Labor Standards Act

Nonagricultural Jobs	Agricultural Employment
Regulations governing youth employment in nonfarm jobs differ somewhat from those pertaining to agricultural employment. In nonfarm work, the permissible jobs and hours of work, by age, are as follows: (1) Persons 18 years or older may perform any job, whether hazardous or not, for unlimited hours; (2) Youths 16 and 17 years old may perform any nonhazardous job, for unlimited hours; and (3) Within limits, youths 14 and 15 years old may work in retail stores, food service establishments, and gasoline service stations. They can work no more than 3 hours on a school day, 18 hours in a school week, 8 hours on a nonschool day, or 40 hours in a nonschool week. Work may not begin before 7 a.m. or end after 7 p.m., except from June 1 through Labor Day, when evening hours are extended to 9 p.m. Fourteen is the minimum age for most nonfarm work. However, at any age, youth may deliver newspapers; perform in radio, television, movie, or theatrical productions; work for parents in their own nonfarm business (except in manufacturing or on hazardous jobs); or, gather evergreens and make evergreen wreaths.	In farmwork, permissible jobs and hours of work by age, are as follows: (1) Youths 16 years and older may perform any job, whether hazardous or not, for unlimited hours; (2) Youths 14 and 15 years old may perform any nonhazardous farm job outside of school hours; (3) Youths 12 and 13 years old may work outside of school hours in nonhazardous jobs, either with a parent's written consent or on the same farm as the parent(s); (4) Youths under 12 years old may perform jobs on farms owned or operated by parent(s), or with a parent's written consent, outside of school hours in nonhazardous jobs on farms not covered by minimum wage requirements.[a] Children of any age are allowed to work on a farm owned or operated by their parents.

Source: Material in this table has been excerpted from the *Handy Reference Guide to the Fair Labor Standards Act*, published by the U.S. Department of Labor, Employment Standards

Administration, Wage and Hour Division, WH Publication 1282, Revised October 1996. See Title 29 C.F.R, Part 570, for a more complete explanation of child labor regulation.

a. The "not covered by minimum wage" provision limits the exemption, effectively, to small farms.

Some have urged nonparental oversight. Academic problems or frequent truancy could indicate oppressive child labor; but, do school authorities have the time and resources to monitor the work arrangements of their students? When physicians treat young persons for problems that might be work-related, can they reasonably be expected to contact the child's employer or inspect working conditions? Efforts in these directions, early in the century, were often unsuccessful but systems of work permits — sometimes linking school attendance and performance to employment — continue to be urged, together with work injury reporting.

Hazardous Occupations Orders

Under the FLSA, manufacturing and mining work is deemed too hazardous for persons under 18 years of age. However, the Secretary may, at his or her discretion, designate other types of work as similarly too hazardous for persons under 18. In such cases, the Secretary will issue "hazardous occupations orders" or HOs which are incorporated in the Code of Federal Regulations (see Table 2).

Often, an exception will be made (and written into the HO) with respect to apprentices and student-learners. The regulations make clear that, where there is a conflict between the HOs and any other provision of law, the higher standard prevails. Each HO is precise, frequently responding to problems that have arisen in the workplace. Currently, there are 17 HOs in place with respect to nonagricultural employment and include (among others) occupations such as work involving "manufacturing or storing explosives," "operation of power-driven meat-processing machines and occupations involving slaughtering, meat packing or processing, or rendering," and "logging occupations and occupations in the operation of any sawmill, lath mill, shingle mill, or cooperage stock mill." Eleven HOs have been published with respect to agricultural employment (see **Table 3**, below). Changes in the HOs or HOAs often invoke close oversight by the Congress.[30]

Table 2. Hazardous Occupations Orders Issued by the Secretary of Labor: Work Generally Unsuitable for Certain Young Persons

C.F.R.	Type of Work
HO 1 (29 C.F.R. § 570.51)	Occupations in or about plants or establishments manufacturing or storing explosives or articles containing explosive components.
HO 2 (29 C.F.R. § 570.52)	Occupations of motor-vehicle driver and outside helper.
HO 3 (29 C.F.R. § 570.53)	Coal mine occupations.
HO 4 (29 C.F.R. § 570.54)	Logging occupations and occupations in the operation of any sawmill, lath mill, shingle mill, or cooperage stock mill.
HO 5 (29 C.F.R. § 570.55)	Occupations involved in the operation of power-driven wood-working machines.
HO 6 (29 C.F.R. § 570.56)	Exposure to radioactive substances and to ionizing radiations.
HO 7 (29 C.F.R. § 570.58)	Occupations involved in the operation of power-driven hoisting apparatus.
HO 8 (29 C.F.R. § 570.59)	Occupations involved in the operations of power-driven metal forming, punching, and shearing machines.
HO 9 (29 C.F.R. § 570.60)	Occupations in connection with mining, other than coal.
HO 10 (29 C.F.R. § 570.61)	Occupations in the operation of power-driven meat-processing machines and occupations involving slaughtering, meat packing or processing, or rendering.
HO 11 (29 C.F.R. § 570.62)	Occupations involved in the operation of bakery machines.
HO 12 (29 C.F.R. § 570.63)	Occupations involved in the operation of paper-products machines.
HO 13 (29 C.F.R. § 570.64)	Occupations involved in the manufacture of brick, tile, and kindred products.
HO 14 (29 C.F.R. § 570.65)	Occupations involved in the operations of circular saws, band saws, and guillotine shears.
HO 15 (29 C.F.R. § 570.66)	Occupations involved in wrecking, demolition, and shipbreaking operations.
HO 16 (29 C.F.R. § 570.67)	Occupations in roofing operations.
HO 17 (29 C.F.R. § 570.68)	Occupations in excavation operations.

Note: Each of these Hazardous Occupation Orders is developed in detail in the Code of Federal Regulations with specific qualifying factors explained.

RE-EMERGENCE OF THE CHILD LABOR ISSUE (1982-2000)

By the late 1940s, exploitation and endangerment of young children in the world of work was popularly believed to have been resolved through legislation (the FLSA) and through the administrative discretion of the Secretary of Labor in implementing the FLSA. But, occasionally, someone would recall that very young children still toiled in field harvest work or an especially egregious accident would bring the more general issue back to the front page.

At the same time, there had begun a gradual shift of focus to a new issue — inadequate opportunities for youth employment — and the related question of delinquency. In May 1961, for example, some 500 men and women met in Washington "to discuss [this] ... serious but little known national problem." The summary report of the conference observed that

> Again and again in the past decade, juvenile delinquency and the outbreaks of youthful street gangs have made headlines. The fact that large numbers of our youth, 16 to 21 years of age, are out of school and unemployed, significant as it may be in terms of delinquency, has far greater significance in terms of what changes are taking place in our society....

The summary report pointed to an unemployment rate of 17.1% for this age group — with a somewhat higher rate for minority youth. "There have always been young people who dropped out before finishing high school or grade school.... But until recently, except during the depression, there were ample unskilled jobs for workers of limited education." That, the report stated, was no longer true. "When no work is to be had at home, the small-town boys and the farm boys go off to the cities where, ill-prepared for urban jobs, they swell the ranks of the young unemployed." And that, argued Harvard's James B. Conant, "is *social dynamite*" (emphasis in the original).[31]

Through the next two decades, the literature on youth employment (youth joblessness) grew rapidly with numerous panaceas for the problem being advanced. In retrospect, there seems to have been little agreement among policy analysts — except that the problem was serious.[32] However, youth unemployment (or joblessness) notwithstanding, large numbers of youths have continued to seek and to find work.

Table 3. Hazardous Occupations Orders Issued by the Secretary of Labor: Work Unsuitable for Young Persons Under 16 Years of Age Employed in Agriculture

Order Number	Type of Work
HOA 1	Operating a tractor of over 20 horsepower, or connecting or disconnecting an implement or any of its parts to or from such a tractor.
HOA 2	Operating or assisting to operate (including starting, stopping, adjusting, feeding, or any other activity involving physical contact associated with the operation) any of the following machines: • Corn picker, cotton picker, grain combine, hay mower, forage harvester, hay baler, potato digger, or mobile pea viner; • Feed grinder, crop dryer, forage blower, auger conveyor, or the unloading mechanism of a nongravity-type self-unloading wagon or trailer; or • Power post-hole digger, power post driver, or nonwalking type rotary tiller.
HOA 3	Operating or assisting to operate (including starting, stopping, adjusting, feeding, or any other activity involving physical contact associated with the operation) any of the following machines: • Trencher or earthmoving equipment; • Fork lift; • Potato combine; or • Power-driven circular, band, or chain saw.
HOA 4	Working on a farm in a yard, pen, or stall occupied by a: • Bull, boar, or stud horse maintained for breeding purposes; or • Sow with suckling pigs, or cow with newborn calf (with umbilical cord present).
HOA 5	Felling, bucking, skidding, loading, or unloading timber with a diameter of more than 6 inches.
HOA 6	Working from a ladder or scaffold (e.g., painting, repairing, or building structures, pruning trees, or picking fruit) at a height of over 20 feet.
HOA 7	Driving a bus, truck, or automobile when transporting passengers, or riding on a tractor as a passenger or helper.
HOA 8	Working inside: • A fruit, forage, or grain storage designed to retain an oxygen deficient or toxic atmosphere; • An upright silo within two weeks after silage has been added or when a top unloading device is in the operating position; • A manure pit; or • A horizontal silo while operating a tractor for packing purposes.
HOA 9	Handling or applying (including cleaning or decontaminating equipment, disposal or return of empty containers, or serving as a flagman for aircraft applying) agricultural chemicals classified toxic, identified by the word "poison" and the "skull and crossbones" on the label, or identified by the word "warning" on the label.
HOA 10	Handling or using a blasting agent, including but not limited to, dynamite, black powder, sensitized ammonium nitrate, blasting caps, and primer cord.
HOA 11	Transporting, transferring, or applying anhydrous ammonia.

Source: 29 C.F.R., Parts 570-571.

Many young persons under the age 15 are employed, but surveys have only commenced to assess their work patterns.[33] However, an absence of data ought not to be construed to imply that persons younger than 15 years of age are not employed. The extent of their employment and the socioeconomic circumstances of their lives may be open to speculation.

Employment of older youth, however, is better understood. Looking at labor force participation by 15- to 17-year-old-youth through the period 1996-1998, on average, "about a fourth of both male and female youths were employed during average school months. During the summer, about one-third of both male and female youths worked," the Department of Labor reported. But DOL also reported significant variations in employment status when considered in terms of race and ethnicity. About 28% of white youths were employed during school months; about 38% during the summer. For blacks, the comparable figures were 13% (school months) and 20% (summer); for youth of Hispanic origin, 15% (school months), 20% (summer).[34]

The Reagan-Era Initiatives

In July 1982, Labor Secretary Raymond Donovan (for the Reagan Administration) proposed that existing child labor policy be updated. The Administration's plan would have: (a) opened more opportunities for employment for children 14 and 15 years of age; (b) extended the number of hours per day and per week that children might be employed; (c) revised standards for the employment of child workers in jobs once considered too hazardous; and (d) simplified and broadened the manner in which employers could become certified by DOL to employ full-time students at less than the standard minimum wage.

The Donovan proposal sparked an immediate reaction. When opening hearings before the House Labor Standards Subcommittee of which he was chair, Representative George Miller (D-CA) sharply criticized the Administration's proposals.[35] In turn, Wage/Hour Administrator William Otter defended them as sound and reasonable public policy. He read from letters from young persons, parents and potential employers urging flexibility in child labor regulation so that 14- and 15-year-olds could be more easily employed. Although acknowledging a high unemployment rate among 16- to 19-year-olds, Otter affirmed his concern "about the unemployment levels of all age groups" and stated the view that "[u]nreasonable and artificial impediments to the employment of all age groups should be eliminated."[36]

Proponents and critics seemed to agree that the Reagan Administration "had walked into a minefield" where the child labor issue was concerned.[37] In February 1983, *Nation's Restaurant News* reported that "Federal wage and hour regulators are sifting through a blizzard of letters from restaurant operators across the nation supporting the Reagan Administration's plan to relax child labor restrictions on the employment of young teenagers in food-service outlets." But, the *News* also reported that the proposal had "generated a storm of protest from educational groups, labor unions, and Congressmen who expressed outrage over what some described as a scheme to enable restauranteurs to exploit school age workers."[38]

For a time, the regulations remained under review with periodic speculation that their release was imminent. In the spring of 1984, the *Nation's Restaurant News* speculated that they would likely appear "by the end of the year."[39] Later, it was reported that the proposal was "likely to resurface" in the near future.[40] But, after a year, it was noted that DOL was again delaying "action on a regulation governing the employment of minors between the ages of 14 and 16."[41] Some suggested "a politically inspired delay" in release of a final rule.[42] Whatever the cause, a final revision never appeared.

Controversies and Changes of Law

As the Reagan Administration proposals receded ever further into the background, several committees of the Congress conducted hearings on aspects of child labor — a process that would continue, intermittently, through the 1 980s and 1990s. But, although they established an evidentiary record, no general legislation restructuring child labor law was approved.

In 1987, Labor Secretary William Brock announced formation of a Child Labor Advisory Committee to assist him with interpretation of child labor issues. The Committee was chaired by Linda Golodner who was also executive director of the National Consumers' League. The advisory body quickly concluded that child labor was "often on the low end of the priority list" at DOL and that it took "very, very long for [its] ... recommendations to get through the bureaucracy." In the spring of 1989, the Department explained that the suggestions of the Committee had, gradually, moved through four lower levels of review and that, by mid-May, they had reached the desk of the Administrator of the Wage and Hour Division.[43]

Administrative changes in the wake of the 1988 election may have caused further delay in moving forward with child labor issues. With the appointment of Elizabeth Dole as Secretary of Labor (January 1989), the Department appeared to have adopted a more active interest in the child labor issue. In mid-1989, Secretary Dole announced appointment of William Brooks of General Motors to serve as Assistant Secretary for Employment Standards and charged him, inter alia, with child labor issues.[44]

Almost at once, the new assistant secretary was confronted with a GAO report affirming that child labor violations had increased dramatically during recent years. But GAO also suggested that data concerning work (and injuries) involving young persons were not entirely satisfactory. A more nearly adequate database was needed.[45]

Departmental initiatives, with investigations by GAO and the Consumers' League, combined with existing congressional concern to give the issue of child labor enhanced visibility. In early 1990, Brooks informed the Advisory Committee that a special task force on child labor would be formed within DOL and would look into such issues as possible revision of the hazardous work orders and the penalty structure for child labor violations. Brooks promised, the *Daily Labor Report* reported, "that in the next six months, rigorous enforcement of child labor law will be the watchword of the agency."[46] Hearings followed, along with new legislative proposals. And, DOL launched *Operation Child Watch,* the first in a series of "sweeps" or general inspections aimed at compliance.[47] Changes were made in the penalty structure and, presumably, in DOL's enforcement policy.

Some viewed DOL's initiatives as a "commendable start" — but there were also misgivings. Representative Don Pease (D-OH), one of the more outspoken advocates of child labor reform, argued that something more was needed than "occasional public relations events" and intermittent crack-downs on violators. Although Pease seems to have favored legislative reform, the Bush Administration apparently did not.[48] In June 1990, Brooks assured the National Grocers Association that no new legislation was necessary: that any needed changes "can be made administratively."[49] The status of the Advisory Committee was unclear. Golodner reported in November of 1990 that no meeting of the Committee had been held since early in the year, that the terms of current members had expired in March, and that no new members had been named by DOL. In late 1990, Secretary Dole indicated her intent to retire. Brooks resigned to return to General Motors.[50]

In 1994, the Clinton Administration proposed a general review of child labor regulation, similar in scope to that proposed by Secretary Donovan, though of a different thrust. Comprehensive oversight and administrative reform continued to be discussed but, essentially, both Congress and DOL proceeded on an ad hoc basis.

The "Bat Boy" Issue

In April 1986, Senator Dan Quayle (R-IN) proposed that child labor law be relaxed to permit 14- and 15-year-olds to work as bat boys or bat girls for professional baseball team, even when games might run until late at night. The Senator stated that baseball "is the All-American sport" and indicated that youngsters should not be forced to wait until they were 16 years of age "to associate with the players of their home town teams."[51] Congress mandated a study of the question, and the issue was allowed to die.

In the spring of 1993, the matter was raised again when it prevented a 14-yearold youngster from Georgia from serving as a bat boy for the Savannah Cardinals. Labor Secretary Robert Reich, faced with the difficulty of explaining the logic of the work hours requirement, suspended its enforcement and proposed to allow children of 14 and 15 years of age to work as late as circumstances might dictate — "before, during, and after a sporting event," around the playing field, "club house or locker room" — to provide "sports-attending services at professional sporting events." Certain conditions were specified, intended to protect children from hazardous activity. And thus, by the spring of 1995, the regulation had been changed.[52]

But questions remained. For example, if it were inappropriate, per se, for young persons (14 and 15 years of age) to work late hours on a school night, did it really matter what sort of work they were doing? How did "sports-attending services" differ, in that context, from work in the food services industry or in a real estate or law office entering data into a computer? Might a more routine business environment be preferable to that of professional sports for the education and welfare of 14- and 15-year-olds? Some in the restaurant industry argued that "it was unfair to exempt the sports industry from the hours and time restrictions while leaving the restrictions in place for all other employment."[53]

Paper Balers and Compactors

Under Hazardous Occupations Order No. 12, persons under 18 were not allowed to load waste paper and boxes into commercial (industrial) paper balers and compactors. Operation of such equipment, DOL had determined, was especially hazardous for younger workers. Even loading them was viewed by the Department as a serious risk. Karen Keesling, Acting Administrator of DOL's Wage and Hour Division, explained that it was not just the loading but that individuals involved in that process would likely reach into a baler or compactor to keep the materials from falling out or to clear jammed materials — and "that is extremely hazardous."[54] Conversely, the National Grocers Association termed HO 12 "a prime example of regulatory excess."[55]

In March 1995, Representative Thomas Ewing (R-IL) introduced H.R. 1114, legislation that would have permitted operation of the baling/compacting machinery by "minors under 18 years of age" — so long as the equipment met safety standards established by the private sector American National Standards Institute (ANSI). A similar proposal was introduced by Senator Larry Craig (R-ID). The legislation was supported by the National Grocers Association and opposed by the Child Labor Coalition (a youth advocacy group) and by people in the trade union movement. As signed into law (P.L. 104-174) on August 6, 1996, the legislation had been redrawn to permit workers "who are 16 and 17 years of age ... to load materials into, but not operate or unload materials from, scrap paper balers and paper box compactors" that meet ANSI safety standards and where certain other requirements have been met. Whether the qualifying language was adequate to protect the youthful workers, however, remained in dispute.[56]

Work-Related Operation of Motor Vehicles

Hazardous Occupations Order No. 2, as developed at the discretion of the Secretary of Labor, restricted the work-related operation of certain motor vehicles by persons under the age of 18 as "particularly hazardous" for younger workers. While not absolutely precluded, strict guidelines and limitations had to be complied with. Conformity with specified safety standards and operation only during daylight hours was required. Employment- related driving could only be "occasional and incidental" though there might be some doubt about the definition of such terms.

In April 1994, Representative Mike Kreidler (D-WA) introduced legislation directing the Secretary to modify HO 2 to permit a wider opportunity for young persons to drive in conjunction with their regular work. No action was taken on the Kreidler bill and in July 1995, new legislation was introduced by Representative Randy Tate (R-WA) and Senator Slade Gorton (R-WA). Hearings followed but the legislation died at the close of the 104th Congress. In July 1997, Representative Larry Combest (R-TX) reintroduced the issue as H.R. 2327 (the Drive for Teen Employment Act).

Though modification of HO 2 had been endorsed by automobile dealers, it had been opposed by the Department of Labor and by groups associated with children's advocacy such as the Child Labor Coalition and the National

Consumers League. Persons 16 and 17 years of age, normally, are beginning drivers who will have only recently qualified for a driver's licence. Although some youngsters may be fine drivers, it was argued that their lack of experience created a significant risk, both to the young persons themselves and to the public.

In its final form, the legislation proposed to allow persons 17 years of age to engage in limited professional driving, under specified safety conditions and with certain limitations, but would still prohibit such activity by persons under 17. The Combest bill, as amended, was signed by President Clinton on October 31, 1998 (P.L. 105-334).[57]

CHILD LABOR INITIATIVES DURING THE 108TH CONGRESS

Child labor concerns have, generally, been a mixture of economic and social policy. Although Congress and DOL, at least for now, have resolved certain aspects of child labor regulations, other and often broader issues remain.

The Traveling Sales Crew Protection Act

On September 23, 2003, Representative Tom Lantos (D-CA) introduced H.R. 3139, the Youth Worker Protection Act, one component of which was the provision that "No employer may employ a minor [a person under 18 years of age] in youth peddling." The bill, which went on to define what is included within the concept of "peddling," was referred to the Committee on Education and the Workforce and, in mid-October 2003, to the Subcommittee on Workforce Protections.

Some Questions of Public Policy

Periodically through recent years, concerns have been raised about the welfare of young persons (the age varies) who are engaged in certain types of outside sales work. On occasion, the focus has been upon the "street trades": selling newspapers, candy, or other items at subway stops or, locally, from door-to-door. In such cases, a manager or supervisor may recruit young persons, move them to various local sites and, at day's end, collect them and bring them back to their homes. But, there is also another arrangement: the "traveling sales crews" in which a sales team goes on the road and remains away from its home base, possibly for extended periods. Some argue that each of these types of sales ("peddling") can encompass risks, especially for young persons.

Such sales work by young persons suggests numerous questions of public policy. For example, how young is too young for children to be engaged in street sales, potentially in rough neighborhoods with which they may not be familiar? And, if they do engage in such work, through what hours should they be employed: how early in the morning and how late at night?

The situation becomes more complicated when groups of recruits are transported from their homes to a distant city to engage in sales work. Are the vehicles in which they are transported safe and insured? How and where are these workers housed? Does the manager or supervisor have authority and responsibility with respect to the off-hours behavior of these young workers? What happens if one of these young persons becomes ill and needs medical attention?

Beyond the personal, there are strictly workplace questions. What is the employment relationship between these workers and the manager or supervisor? Are the youth workers employees, independent contractors, or something else entirely? To the extent that they are employees, by whom are they employed? The manager or supervisor may also be an employee of some more distant entity. Where does responsibility ultimately reside? How are wages and benefits handled? What employment records are maintained — and by whom?

From a policy perspective, some may ask: Should young persons be excluded, by law, from working in street or door-to-door sales or in related support services other than actual selling? Were otherwise applicable hours restrictions to be observed, would such work be acceptable? Would a blanket prohibition on outside sales work by persons under 18 years of age unduly restrict their capacity to earn? Is there something inherently inappropriate about street sales or door-to-door sales? Is such work wrong when 16- and 17-year-olds are involved, but a legitimate entrepreneurial activity if all of the sales staff (and, perhaps, support staff) are 18 and over? Is such work acceptable when confined to a certain radius from the permanent residence of the sales staff? And, how expansive should that radius be?

The Wyden Initiative

In May 1985 (the 99th Congress), then-Representative Ron Wyden (D-OR), stating that "unscrupulous door-to-door selling groups" were exploiting young persons (some of them, children; others, young adults), introduced legislation to establish a National Clearinghouse on Fraudulent Youth Employment Practices. While Wyden conceded that "the vast majority of door-to-door sellers are wholly honorable and reputable," others, he suggested, were not. These companies "can be peddling anything from magazine subscriptions to chemical cleaners." He outlined a host of alleged violations of law and fraudulent sales practices engaged in by such firms and urged his colleagues to help "put these dangerous and unscrupulous operators out of business. And ... take a step toward protecting our youth from dangerous employment practices."[58]

Hearings were conducted (November 1985) by the House Subcommittee on Civil and Constitutional Rights. Susan Meisinger, speaking for the Reagan Labor Department, testified that there was indeed a problem. "Unlawful practices reported by the States include violations of their child labor laws, violations of minimum wage laws, employer failure to pay taxes and unemployment insurance, and abuse of child workers," Meisinger noted, "including forcing them to pay kickbacks, child molesting, and placing them in high risk, late night employment environments."[59]

But the Reagan Administration was divided on the issue. Victoria Toensing, representing the Department of Justice, agreed that "problems relating to the recruitment and use of salespersons do exist" but she suggested that any legislative action would be premature. "The extent of these problems has not yet been established," Toensing stated, and, in any case, state and local authorities "may be as effective, if not more so, than the federal government in preventing such abuses." Further, she suggested, not all of the alleged worker/victims were minors. After reviewing a series of federal statutes that might apply if there actually were a problem, Toensing noted that the Department of Justice "... considers present statutory provisions adequate."[60]

The Wyden bill (H.R. 2544) died at the close of the 99th Congress. Hearings on the general issue were subsequently conducted by the Senate Permanent Subcommittee on Investigations (1987)[61] and by the House Committee on Government Operations' Subcommittee on Employment and Housing (1990).[62] In each case, the matter was restricted to general oversight. Further legislation was not then proposed.[63]

The Kohl Proposals

In November 1999 (the 106th Congress), Senator Kohl introduced S. 1989, the Traveling Sales Crew Protection Act — his interest sparked by an auto accident in Wisconsin in which seven young people were killed and others injured. The Senator explained: "The driver [in the Wisconsin case] had a suspended license and a series of violations." These firms, he stated, "employ crews who travel from city to city selling products door to door. Often times," he asserted, "... [they] mistreat their workers and violate local, state, and federal labor law. Because they rapidly move from state to state, enforcement efforts are difficult if not impossible for local authorities." Senator Kohl recalled that it had been 12 years since the hearing by the Permanent Subcommittee on Investigations (noted above) and affirmed: "... nothing has changed. These abuses continue, and Congress should act."[64] But, no action was taken: the bill died at the close of the 106th Congress.

Early in the 107th Congress, Senator Kohl introduced new traveling sales crew/peddling legislation (S. 96). The Kohl bill would have amended the FLSA to provide that "No individual under 18 years of age may be employed in a position requiring the individual to engage in door to door sales or in related support work in a manner that requires the individual to remain away from his or her permanent residence for more than 24 hours." After defining the operative language, the bill set forth a registration requirement for employers and supervisors of traveling sales crew workers. Then, assuming that such practices were to be allowed, it outlined the obligations of the parties — dealing with such issues as housing, transportation, wages (and deductions therefrom), insurance, and related matters. It then proposed a system for enforcement.

A comprehensive and detailed proposal, S. 96 was referred to the Committee on Health, Education, Labor and Pensions (HELP) where no action was taken.[65] Then, on May 22, 2002, Senator Kohl introduced S. 2549, an abbreviated version of the traveling sales crew/peddling legislation. An amendment to Section 12 of the FLSA, S. 2549 read, in pertinent part:

> No individual under 18 years of age may be employed in a position requiring the individual to engage in door to door sales or in related support work in a manner that requires the individual to remain away from his or her permanent residence for more than 24 hours.

It further authorized the Secretary of Labor to "issue such rules and regulations as are necessary to carry out" the proposed amendment. On August 1, 2002, the HELP Committee, to which the bill had been referred, was discharged from further consideration and the bill, under unanimous consent, was agreed to by the Senate.[66] It was referred to the House Committee on

Education and the Workforce, Subcommittee on Workforce Protections, where it died at the close of the 107th Congress.

The issue was raised in the 108th Congress, again in an abbreviated form, with introduction of H.R. 2139 by Representative Lantos: an umbrella child labor reform proposal, discussed below. No action, however, was taken on the Lantos bill.[67] In the 109th Congress, Lantos again introduced the issue as part of H.R. 2870, a general bill dealing with child labor. But once more, the bill was directed to the Subcommittee on Workforce Protections, where it remained.

Sawmilling/Woodworking by 14-Year-Olds

On May 1, 2003, legislation to permit employment of young persons (of at least 14 years of age) in sawmilling and woodworking facilities was introduced by Representative Joseph Pitts (R-PA) and Senator Arlen Specter (R-PA) — respectively H.R. 1943 and S. 974. On October 8, 2003, a hearing on the Pitts bill was conducted by the House Subcommittee on Workforce Protections.

A Question of Public Policy

Work in or around sawmills and woodworking machinery has been deemed by DOL as especially hazardous for persons under 18 years of age. The practice violates at least two Departmental Hazardous Occupations (HO) Orders: HO 4, covering sawmills, and HO 5, dealing with power-driven woodworking machines.[68]

Speaking generally, the Amish resist requirements of law that would alter their traditional way of life and have rejected compulsory school attendance beyond the 8th grade. The *Daily Labor Report* explains: "After completing their formal classroom training [elementary school] at age 14 or 15, Amish boys typically receive training in farming or carpentry from their fathers."[69] In recent years, the opportunity for the Amish to farm has diminished — in part, because of increased land values and property taxes. Therefore, the Amish have sought other activities for their children. "What are we supposed to do with them if they don't work here," lamented one member of the Amish community, "have them stay on the street all day?"[70]

The Amish have sought to have their sons work in sawmills and woodworking plants where there is Amish supervision (or where they are supervised by an adult relative).[71] The Department of Labor has held that permitting children to work in such plants would be a violation of federal child labor law: HO 4 and HO 5. The result has been a clash between the Amish and DOL. The Amish have pressed for an amendment to the child labor provisions of the FLSA in order to accommodate their practices.

Taking the Issue to Congress

At least since the 105th Congress, legislation to amend federal child labor law on behalf of the Amish has been repeatedly introduced, both in the House and in the Senate. The bills, generally, would widen the opportunity for youth ages 14 to 18 "to be employed inside or outside places of business where machinery is used to process wood products." In order to qualify for such employment, a youth would have to be "a member of a religious sect or division thereof whose established teachings do not permit formal education beyond the eighth grade." In the 105th and 106th Congresses, the Amish legislation was passed by the House under suspension but the Senate did not act.[72]

Had the legislation been adopted, Amish children, having left school after the 8th grade, could have been employed in work otherwise regarded as too hazardous for persons under 18 years of age. Some have suggested that constitutional issues may be involved in affording special treatment to the Amish that is not afforded to other religious groups. Setting aside issues of legality, other questions could be raised, given that Amish children are permitted to leave school after the 8th grade.[73] First, would elimination of federal restrictions upon child labor — to the extent proposed in the legislation — provide an opportunity (and, perhaps, an incentive) for Amish children to leave school and to enter the world of work? Or, would it merely recognize that Amish children are already out of school and, thus, permit them to be productively occupied? Second, assuming that these children do leave school to work, are sawmills and wood processing establishments appropriate places of employment for any youngsters under the age of 18? Might other areas of skills training be more suitable for children than mill work with its attendant hazards? What types of work are suitable for 14-year-old Amish children and who should decide?[74]

In order to strengthen the ties of Amish children to the Amish community, youngsters are systematically separated from the non-Amish world.[75] The work experience of Amish children with the skills they acquire on the family farm may not be readily transferable to the non-Amish marketplace. Thus, with only an eighth grade education and lacking experience in the non-Amish world, their subsequent choices may be, accordingly, restricted, rendering their out-migration from the community within which they were raised extremely difficult.[76] Some may applaud this result; others may question the appropriateness of a federal role in its facilitation.

On May 3, 2001, the Senate Appropriations Subcommittee on Labor, Health and Human Services, and Education, conducted an oversight hearing on the employment needs of Amish youth. Representative Mark Souder (R-IN) spoke in support of exemption. Mr. Souder, representing a partly Amish constituency, explained that the Amish had not been able to persuade DOL to acquiesce in industrial employment for Amish children at age 14. Urging amendment of the FLSA to permit such employment, he argued that the Amish children would be "supervised by adults who know and care about them" and that the proposed amendment "would protect a truly endangered religion and culture."[77]

Thomas M. Markey of DOL testified in opposition, arguing: "Sawmills are dangerous places to work, even for adults." Pointing to a high accident and fatality rate for the industry nationwide, he stated that such work is "even more dangerous for children."[78]

On June 13, 2001, during consideration of S. 1 (reauthorization of the Elementary and Secondary Education Act), Senator Specter proposed S.Amdt. 420. It would have amended the FLSA to permit Amish youngsters, 14 years of age and older, to work, under specified conditions, in mills and woodworking plants. Senator Edward M. Kennedy (D-MA), chairman of the Committee on Health, Education, Labor, and Pensions (HELP), and Senator Specter engaged in a brief debate. Senator Kennedy affirmed that it "would be valuable to have ... an open hearing" on the issue — particularly with respect to the safety of prospective workers — and agreed that his committee would conduct such a hearing. With that understanding, Senator Specter then withdrew his proposed amendment.[79]

On July 25, 2001, legislation to permit Amish youth to work at age 14 in wood processing plants was introduced both in the House and in the Senate: H.R. 2639 (Pitts) and S. 1241 (Specter). No action was taken on these proposals.

Revived in the 108th Congress

The Pitts (H.R. 1943) and Specter (S. 974) bills of the 108th Congress largely follow the pattern of recent years. To be exempt from the restraints of federal child labor law, several standards would be imposed. The targeted youth must be "at least 14" years of age. Further, the child:

(a) Must be "by statute or judicial order ... exempt from compulsory school attendance beyond the eighth grade."[80]
(b) Must be "supervised by an adult relative" or "by an adult member of the same religious sect or division as the individual."
(c) May not "operate or assist in the operation of power-driven woodworking machines."
(d) Must be "protected from wood particles or other flying debris within the workplace by a barrier appropriate to the potential hazard of such wood particles or flying debris or by maintaining a sufficient distance from machinery in operation..."
(e) "[I]is required to use personal protective equipment to prevent exposure to excessive levels of noise and saw dust."

Other concerns aside, some may ask: Would the safeguards be adequate? In the absence of frequent DOL inspections, would the precautions be observed? Does the fact that a supervisor would be of "the same religious sect" as the child worker render the work any less hazardous — or the supervisor any more diligent in monitoring the youth's work?

On October 8, 2003, the Subcommittee on Workforce Protections conducted a hearing on H.R. 1943. In an opening statement, Chairman Charlie Norwood (R-GA) observed that the bill provides:

> ... that certain youth whose religious faith and beliefs dictate that they "learn by doing" are afforded an opportunity to do so, and that the federal government — however well-meaning — does not endanger the belief and culture of these young people and their families.[81]

As the lead witness (DOL was not represented at the hearing), Representative Pitts stated that actions of the Department had "severely threatened the lifestyle and religion of this respected and humble community" and averred that the "government should not interfere" with Amish practices lest "their strong heritage ... be undermined."[82] Representative Mark Souder (R-IN), while reviewing the proposed safeguards embodied in the amendment, also framed the issue in religious terms. Government bureaucracy, he stated, "... is threatening the Amish people's very way of life. It is interfering with their religious freedom."[83] Christ K. Blank, speaking for the Old Order Amish, concurred, declaring "the ages 14 through 17 to be a very tender receptive age" and a period during which "to instill ... Amish values and work ethics in our children."[84]

But, not all were in complete agreement. Nicholas Clark of the United Food and Commercial Workers, AFL-CIO, recognized the religious desires of the Amish community. He pointed out, however, that federal government studies had found that working conditions in "sawmilling and woodworking are among the most hazardous occupations for adults, with a death rate that is *five times* the national average for all industries," and that such work is "especially inappropriate for young workers" (emphasis in the original). Clark expressed concern about constitutional issues and raised, as well, the issue of equity. The proposed amendment "... would grant Amish-owned sawmills and woodworking firms an exception from child labor laws that are [sic] denied firms owned by persons of non-Amish faiths." Further, he argued, it would deny "Amish children the very real benefits of governmental health and safety protections that are afforded Catholic, Baptist, Jewish or any other" non-Amish children. While sawmills and woodworking plants "provide much needed employment for Amish adults," he concluded, "they cannot safely or constitutionally serve that purpose for Amish children."[85]

Amish Child Workers and the 2004 Appropriations Bill

As the first session of the 108th Congress moved to a close, several appropriations bills (among them, the measure providing funding for the Department of Labor) remained to be passed. Ultimately, the several appropriations bills were combined in H.R. 2673, the FY2004 Consolidated Appropriations bill.

A conference report on H.R. 2673 (H.Rept. 108-40 1) was filed on November 25, 2003. Included in the conference report (Senator Specter had served as a Senate conferee) was language roughly paralleling that of H.R. 1943, the Amish child labor bill. In an explanation of the measure, the conference report stated:

> The conference agreement includes a provision to permit youth, ages 14 through 17, who by statute or judicial order are exempt from compulsory school attendance beyond the eighth grade, to work inside or outside places of business where machinery is used to process wood products. The youth would be permitted to perform activities such as sweeping, stacking wood, and writing orders. Safety provisions include prohibiting the youth from operating machinery, and requiring the use of eye and body protections.

CHILD LABOR INITIATIVES DURING THE 109TH CONGRESS

As with previous years, child labor remained a subject of interest among some Members of the 109th Congress. Several bills from prior Congresses were reintroduced. Several new bills were added. (See **Table 4**, below.)

Table 4. Child Labor Proposals of the 109th Congress

Bill No.	Sponsor	Action Beyond Referral	Impact
H.R. 1142	Foley	—	To prohibit "exploitive child modeling" involving persons under 17 years of age
H.R. 2870	Lantos	—	A comprehensive overview of child labor with restrictions placed upon child workers: school-to-work transition; prohibition of youth peddling; mandates for reporting requirements; and imposition of certain other restraints
H.R. 3482	Roybal-Allard	—	Focuses upon agricultural child workers.
H.R. 3753	Musgrave	—	Comprehensive home school bill; suggests that "home schooled students" (14 to 16 years of age) be permitted to work longer than hours worked by public school students
H.R. 4190	DeLauro	—	Requires (a) that the Secretary of Labor not pre-disclose an inspection, and (b) that a study and report of child labor issues be made to Congress
S. 1691	Craig	—	See the Musgrave bill (H.R. 3753), above
S. 2357	Kennedy	—	Comprehensive bill (368 pp.) that refers to the restriction of child labor and enforcement of internationally recognized labor standards dealing with child labor

On December 8, 2003, the House voted to approve the conference report (with the Amish child labor provision included). The vote was 242 yeas to 176 nays.[86] Senate consideration of the measure was deferred until the second session of the 108th Congress.[87] On January 20 and 22, the Senate considered the conference report, though attention appears to have focused on overtime pay regulations and subjects other than the Amish child labor provision. On January 22, the Senate approved the conference report by a vote of 65 yeas to 28 nays.[88] The measure was signed by the President on January 23, 2004 (P.L. 108-199).

In a statement to the press, Senator Specter noted that he had "toured an Amish sawmill in Lancaster County, PA," had met with some members of the Amish people, and had come to "know of the importance of this legislation to their community and culture. This is an issue of freedom of religion," he affirmed, "where the Amish prefer to educate their children aside from the public schools and part of that educational process is for teenagers to work in the lumber mills."[89]

Protecting Child Models

On March 8, 2005, the Child Modeling Exploitation Prevention Act (H.R. 1142) was introduced in the House by Representative Mark Foley (R-FL), with others. The bill was referred to the Subcommittee on Workforce Protections of the House Committee on Education and the Workforce and to the Subcommittee on Crime, Terrorism, and Homeland Security of the House Committee on the Judiciary. No further action was taken on the measure.

For a number of years, Representative Foley had raised the issue of children engaged in modeling on Internet sites. "What occurs," he explained in a floor statement, "... is that young girls, 10, 12, 13 years old, are encouraged by their parents and aided and abetted by individuals to display themselves on the Internet for viewer ship, if you will, [by] people who pay a fee, a monthly fee in order to view the site." Although some parents, he suggested, are deceived into thinking that such activity is legitimate modeling, Mr. Foley disagreed. He stated that he was "not suggesting that there is not an appropriate place in commerce for young people to display their talents" but, rather, that he had in mind a particular type of website that encourages "inappropriate" types of modeling by children.[90]

In the 109th Congress, Representative Foley introduced H.R. 1142, which was similar to legislation introduced in the previous Congress (by

Representative Foley in the House and Senator Jim Bunning in the Senate).[91] The proposal amended Section 12 of the FLSA to provide that "no employer may employ a child model in exploitive child modeling." It went on to explain:

(a) In this subsection, the term 'exploitive child modeling' means modeling involving the use of a child under 17 years old for financial gain without the purpose of marketing a product or service other than the image of the child.
(b) Such term applies to any such use, regardless of whether the employment relationship of the child is direct or indirect, or contractual or noncontractual, or is termed that of an independent contractor.

The measure distinguished between an image that is exploitive and one that, "taken as a whole, has serious literary, artistic, political, or scientific value." The legislation proposed both fines and imprisonment (of not more than 10 years) for violators.

Young American Workers' Bill of Rights

General restructuring of the child labor components of the FLSA has long been sought, though from somewhat different perspectives, by industry and by labor. In 1990 (the 101st Congress), Representatives Don Pease (D-OH), Charles Schumer (D-NY) and Tom Lantos (D-CA) introduced legislation titled the "Young American Workers' Bill of Rights." With various changes (but with a continuity of thrust), the legislation would be reintroduced in each Congress thereafter.

In the 109th Congress, the initiatives were set forth in H.R. 2870 (Lantos), the Youth Worker Protection Act. The Lantos bill was comprehensive, providing for a wide variety of changes in current law and practice.[92]

(a) The bill begins by defining a "minor." He or she must be "is at least 14 years old or, if younger than 14 years old, is otherwise permitted to work under this Act." "In the case of a minor who is between the ages of 16 and 18 years, the employment is not in an occupation that is particularly hazardous for the employment of children between those ages or detrimental to their health or wellbeing...." "The minor is employed in accordance with this Act and in accordance with any other Federal, State, or local law that provides greater protection to minors."

(b) The minor has a work permit that includes the specified provisions under this Act.
- The work permit shall include name, date of birth, gender, racial or ethnic background, and contact information for the minor; name, contact information, and consent of a parent of the minor; a certification (if appropriate) by a school official showing attendance requirements; e.g., name, contact information, and type of business of the employer; and type of work.
- The Secretary of Labor will prescribe a unified model for such work permits that will contain information concerning the identity of the child worker and his/her parent (or a similar person where appropriate), contact information and parental consent for the child to work, school status, identification of employer, type of work to be engaged in, name and contact information of the designated state agency, summary of age limitations and other legal requirements for employment of minors, among other information. A system of expiration dates for individual work permits is specified.
- The designated state agency may revoke a work permit if the agency finds either of the following: (1) the minor "is not in compliance with school attendance requirements," or (2) the minor is adversely affected by the employment involved. The minor or the parent of the minor would have had an option for appeal of the revocation.

(c) Hours that are allowable for work by minors were specified in H.R. 2870, together with the number of hours per day and week that can be worked.

(d) If the minor sustains a serious work-related injury, the designated state agency must be notified by each of the following: the employer, the appropriate medical professional, the appropriate law enforcement officer (where applicable), and an employee of the school attended by the minor where an absence of more than three days is involved.[93]

(e) The bill provided that the designated state agency must collect and retain (for seven years) statistical data concerning the work permit system and any work- related injury information.

(f) The designated state agency must report annually to the Secretary of Labor. The report shall include assorted statistical data (see item "e" above) and information concerning "the activities and number of work-hours devoted by State and local government employees (including contractors) to the administration and enforcement of child labor laws in the State."

(g) The bill would have provided that "[no employer may employ a minor in youth peddling" and defines what is included in the concept of youth "peddling." (See discussion of the "peddling" issue, above.)

(h) It set forth extensive requirements for enforcement and penalties.

(i) The bill amended Section 13(c) of the FLSA to raise the age for employment in agriculture outside of school hours from "twelve years of age" to "fourteen years of age."

(j) It makes uniform the standard for employment in hazardous agricultural work.

(k) The bill would repeal the provision of current law permitting, at the discretion of the Secretary (with certain specific criteria), children as young as 10 years of age to work in hand harvest agricultural work.

(l) It would eliminate the employment of children under 18 years of age in connection with commercial paper balers and compactors. (See discussion above.)

(m) "Not later than 24 months after the date of the enactment of this section," the Secretary of Labor is directed to promulgate a rule revising the Hazardous Occupations restraints in certain specified industries. The Secretary was also directed at "appropriate intervals, but in no case less than once during each five- year period," to conduct "a comprehensive review" of the Hazardous Occupations Orders to assure that they are current.

(n) Within 24 months of enactment of this section, the Secretary is directed to promulgate a rule to prohibit employment of minors in (1) seafood processing and (2) employment "requiring a minor to handle or dispose of oil or other liquids from fryers."

(o) Within 36 months, the Secretary was directed to review the employment of minors in work involving: (1) "[r]epetitive bending, stooping, twisting, or squatting," (2) "[l]ifting of heavy and/or unwieldy objects," (3) "[w]orking alone or late at night in retail establishments where there is direct contact with the public and cash is handled," and (4) "[w]ork in the entertainment industry that is detrimental to the health, safety, education or well-being of minors."[94]

> The Secretary shall submit to Congress a report of the review, together with proposed regulations governing such work.

On July 25, 2005, H.R. 2870 was referred to the House Subcommittee on Workforce Protections of the House Committee on Education and the Workforce. The Subcommittee took no action on the bill.

The CARE Act of 2005

For several years, Representative Lucille Roybal-Allard (D-CA) presented legislation that dealt primarily, through not exclusively, with child labor in agriculture. On July 27, 2005, Representative Roybal-Allard introduced H.R. 3482, the Children's Act for Responsible Employment of 2005, or the CARE Act of 2005.

The Roybal-Allard bill began with a revision of Section 13(c), eliminating the option of having young persons under 16 years of age employed in agriculture "including in an agricultural occupation that the Secretary of Labor finds and declares to be particularly hazardous." The bill offered two exceptions: where the employee "is employed by a parent of the employee or by a person standing in the place of the parent," or "on a farm owned or operated by the parent or person" standing in the place of a parent. Further, the bill deleted Section 213(c)(4), which allows an "employer or group of employers" to hire young persons (down to the age of 12 years) for certain select crops.

The bill expanded the penalties, both civil and criminal, for persons found to be in violation of the act. Also, the Secretary of Labor, with respect to persons under 18 years of age employed in agriculture, was to gather data with respect to "each serious lost-time work-related injury, serious lost-time worker-related illness," or work-related death. An employer was expected to submit a report to the Secretary. Failure to file a report was subject to a civil penalty of up to $7,000 per violation. The Secretary could employ at least 100 additional inspectors, whose principal purpose would be to enforce compliance with child labor laws.

The bill provided that the Secretary, not later than 180 days after the date of enactment, would issue rules relating to the exposure of child workers to certain pesticides and related chemicals. It allowed for some measure of accommodation between the Secretary of Labor and the Administrator of the Environmental Protection Agency with respect to pesticide-related fines.

Finally, H.R. 3482 amended the Workforce Investment Act (WIA) of 1998 to provide the greater of $10 million or 4% of the amount appropriated for WIA youth activities for youth activities under the Migrant and Seasonal Farmworker Programs.

The Roybal-Allard bill was referred to the House Committee on Education and the Workforce. On October 12, 2005, it was referred to the Subcommittee on Workforce Protections and to the Subcommittee on 21st Century Competitiveness. The Subcommittee took no action on the bill.

CHILD LABOR INITIATIVES DURING THE 110TH CONGRESS

Several child labor bills have been introduced in the 110th Congress. (See Table 5, below.)

Table 5. Child Labor Proposals of the 110th Congress

Bill No.	Sponsor	Action Beyond Referral	Impact
H.R. 2637	Woolsey	Passed House. Provisions are included in H.R. 493.	Raises the maximum civil penalties for violations of child labor law.
H.R. 2674	Roybal-Allard	—	Focus is on agricultural child workers.
H.R. 6861	Braley	—	Raises the maximum civil penalties and establishes criminal penalties for violations of child labor law.
S. 1598	Coleman	Provisions are included in H.R. 493.	Raises the maximum civil penalties for child labor violations.
S. 1614	Harkin	—	Raises the maximum civil penalties and establishes criminal penalties for violations of child labor law.

The Safe at Work Act

On November 1, 2005, Representative Rosa DeLauro (D-CN) introduced the Safe at Work Act (H.R. 4190). The bill was referred to the House Committee on Education and the Workforce and, on March 24, 2006, to the Subcommittee on Workforce Protections. No action was taken on the proposal.

The DeLauro bill was divided into two parts: First, the bill required that the Secretary of Labor "not enter into any agreement to provide any person with notice prior to commencing an investigation or inspection." Second, it required the Comptroller General to conduct a study of violations of child labor laws "including the number and type of allegations of child labor violations, when and whether inspections or investigations commenced for each such allegation, what enforcement action or other outcome resulted from such inspections or investigations, and a comparison of the extent to which such violations occurred in both large and small businesses...." The time period for the Comptroller General's study was five years prior to the date of enactment.

The Child Labor Protection Act of 2007

Different bills entitled the Child Labor Protection Act of 2007 have been introduced in the current Congress.

In the House, on June 8, 2007, Representative Lynn Woolsey (D-CA) introduced H.R. 2637, which was referred to the Committee on Education and Labor. The House approved the bill by voice vote on June 12, 2007. H.R. 2637 would increase from $10,000 to $11,000 the maximum employer penalty for each employee who is subject to a violation of the child labor provisions of the FLSA. The measure would also establish a maximum civil penalty of $50,000 for each violation that causes the death or serious injury of any employee under the age of 18. The $50,000 penalty may be doubled for repeated or willful violations of child labor law. The bill would also increase from $1,000 to $1,100 the maximum penalty for violating the minimum wage or overtime provisions of the FLSA.

In the Senate, Senator Norm Coleman (R-MN), on June 12, 2007, introduced S. 1598, which was referred to the Committee on Health, Education, Labor, and Pensions (HELP). S. 1598 includes the identical changes in civil penalties as contained in H.R. 2637.

On April 23, 2008, Senator Olympia Snowe (R-ME) introduced an amendment (S.Amdt. 4573) in the nature of a substitute to H.R. 493, the Genetic Information Nondiscrimination Act of 2008. H.R. 493 was approved by the House on April 25, 2007. Senator Snowe's amendment included the provisions of H.R. 2637/S. 1598. The Senate approved the amendment by a vote of 95 in favor and none opposed. The measure was signed into law by President George W. Bush on May 21, 2008, and became P.L. 110-233.

On June 13, 2007, Senator Tom Harkin (D-IA) introduced S. 1614, another version of the Child Labor Protection Act of 2007. S. 1614 would amend the FLSA to establish a minimum civil penalty of $500 and a maximum penalty of $15,000 for each employee who is subject to a child labor violation. The bill would also create a minimum penalty of $ 15,000 and a maximum penalty of $50,000 for each violation of child labor law that causes the death or serious injury of an employee under the age of 18. The latter penalty could be doubled to a maximum of $100,000. The bill would also increase from $1,000 to $1,100 the maximum penalty for violating the minimum wage or overtime provisions of the FLSA. Finally, the measure would establish criminal penalties (fines, imprisonment, or both) for violations of the child labor provisions of the FLSA. The bill was referred to the Senate HELP Committee.

The CARE Act of 2007

On June 12, 2007, Representative Lucille Ms. Roybal-Allard (D-CA) introduced H.R. 2674, the Children's Act for Responsible Employment of 2007, or CARE Act of 2007. Except for two provisions, the measure is the same as the CARE Act of 2005 (H.R. 3482), which was introduced in the 109th Congress. Unlike H.R. 3482, the CARE Act of 2007 does not direct the Secretary of Labor to employ additional inspectors to enforce child labor law. Also, the CARE Act of 2007 would not amend the WIA law with respect to youth activities under the Migrant and Seasonal Farmworker Programs.

H.R. 2674 was referred to the Subcommittee on Workforce Protections of the Education and Labor Committee.

The Child Labor Safety Act

Representative Bruce Braley (D-IA) introduced the Child Labor Safety Act. The act would increase from $11,000 to $50,000 the maximum civil penalty for each employee who is subject to a violation of the child labor provisions of the FLSA. The bill would also raise from $50,000 to $100,000 the maximum penalty for each violation that causes the death or serious injury of any employee under the age of 18. The measure would impose criminal penalties (a maximum fine of $50,000 or imprisonment for up to six months) for violations of child labor law. The bill was introduced on September 10, 2008, and was referred to the Committee on Education and Labor.

End Notes

[1] This report is an update of a CRS report originally written by William G. Whittaker.

[2] This report outlines the basic parameters of the child labor issue. For an authoritative statement of the child labor requirements under the Fair Labor Standards Act, consult 29 C.F.R. Part 570.

[3] An extensive literature exists on child labor in America during the late 19th and early 20th centuries. See, for example Edward N. Clopper, *Child Labor in the City Streets* (New York: The Macmillan Company, 1912); Katharine DuPre Lumpkin, and Dorothy Wolff Douglas, *Child Workers in America* (New York: Robert M. McBride & Company, 1937); Edwin Markham, Benjamin B. Lindsey, and George Creel, *Children In Bondage* (New York: Hearst's International Library Co., 1914); John Spargo, *The Bitter Cry of the Children* (New York: The Macmillan Company, 1906); and John William Larner, Jr., "The Glass House Boys: Child Labor Conditions in Pittsburgh's Glass Factories, 1890-1917," *The Western Pennsylvania Historical Magazine*, October 1965, pp. 355-364.

[4] Robert H. Bremner, *From the Depths: The Discovery of Poverty in the United States* (New York: New York University Press, 1964). Page 218 notes: "The labor unions had been active in the [child labor] movement since the days of the Knights of Labor in the 1880's, and Gompers only slightly exaggerated the facts when he declared [in 1906]: 'There is not a child labor law on the statute books of the United States but has been put there by the efforts of the trade-union movement.'" But, he added: "It is unlikely ... that the campaign against child labor would have made such rapid headway after 1900 had it not been for the pressure brought to bear on both public opinion and legislatures by voluntary groups such as the consumers' leagues, state charities aid associations, federations of women's clubs, and the child-labor committees." See also Samuel Gompers, *Labor and the Common Welfare* (New York: E. P. Dutton & Company, 1919), p. 129; Jeremy P. Felt, *Hostages of Fortune: Child Labor Reform in New York State* (Syracuse: Syracuse University Press, 1965), pp. 10-13, 60, and 196-197; and Roger W. Walker, "The A.F.L. and Child-Labor Legislation: An Exercise in Frustration," *Labor History*, summer 1970, pp. 323-340.

[5] Mary Field Parton (ed.), *The Autobiography of Mother Jones* (Chicago: Charles H. Kerr Publishing Company, 1980), pp. 71-83, 118-131.

[6] Concerning the work of the National Consumers' League, see Josephine Goldmark, *Impatient Crusader* (Urbana: University of Illinois Press, 1953), a biography of Florence Kelley; Kathryn K. Sklar, *Florence Kelley and the Nation's Work*, (New Haven: Yale University

Press, 1995); and Landon R. Y. Storrs, *Civilizing Capitalism: The National Consumers' League, Women's Activism, and Labor Standards in the New Deal Era* (Chapel Hill: University of North Carolina Press, 2000). (Hereafter cited as Storrs, *Civilizing Capitalism.*)

[7] Walter I. Trattner, *Crusade for the Children: A History of the National Child Labor Committee and Child Labor Reform in America* (Chicago: Quadrangle Books, 1970). (Hereafter cited as Trattner, *Crusade for the Children.*) For a discussion of the politics of child labor reform during this early period, see Hugh C. Bailey, *Edgar Gardner Murphy: Gentle Progressive* (Coral Gables: University of Miami Press, 1968), pp. 65-108; and Herbert J. Doherty, Jr., "Alexander J. McKelway: Preacher to Progressive," *Journal of Southern History*, May 1958, pp. 177-190.

[8] Ruth E. Shallcross, *Industrial Homework: An Analysis of Homework Regulations, Here and Abroad* (New York: Industrial Affairs Publishing Co., 1939); Eileen Boris, *Home to Work: Motherhood and the Politics of Industrial Homework in the United States* (New York: Cambridge University Press, 1994); and Ruth Crawford, "Development and Control of Industrial Homework," *Monthly Labor Review*, June 1944, pp. 1145-1158.

[9] John Braeman, "Albert J. Beveridge and the First National Child Labor Bill," *Indiana Magazine of History*, March 1964, pp. 1-36.

[10] U.S. Congress, Senate, 61st Cong., 2nd sess., Document No. 645. *Report on Condition of Woman and Child Wage-Earners in the United States*, 19 Volumes, Washington, U.S. GPO, 1913. See also U.S. Department of Labor, Bureau of Labor Statistics, Women in Industry Series No. 5, *Summary of the Report on Condition of Woman and Child Wage Earners in the United States*, Washington, GPO, 1916, 445 p.

[11] Grace Abbott, "Federal Regulation of Child Labor, 1906-1938," *The Social Service Review*, September 1939, p. 411. (Hereafter cited as Abbott, *Federal Regulation of Child Labor.*)

[12] Trattner, *Crusade for the Children*, pp. 119-138. See also Edward Keating, *The Gentleman from Colorado: A Memoir* (Denver: Sage Books, 1964), pp. 349-355; Lawrence R. Berger, and S. Ryan Johannson, "Child Health in the Workplace: The supreme Court in *Hammer v. Dagenhart* (1918)," *Journal of Health Politics, Policy and Law*, spring 1980, pp. 81-97; Arden J. Lea, "Cotton Textiles and the Federal Child Labor Act of 1916," *Labor History*, fall 1975, pp. 485-494; and Walter I. Trattner, "The First Federal Child Labor Law (1916)," *Social Science Quarterly*, December 1969, pp. 507-524.

[13] Abbott, *Federal Regulation of Child Labor*, p. 416.

[14] Trattner, *Crusade for the Children*, pp. 138-142.

[15] Ibid., pp. 163-186. See also "Now the States Must Act! The Past, the Present and the Future of the Effort to Free American Childhood," *American Federationist*, July 1924, pp. 541-553 — the AFL journal of which Gompers was editor; Vincent A. McQuade, *The American Catholic Attitude on Child Labor Since 1891* (Washington: The Catholic University of America, 1938), pp. 79-100, and 112-128; Thomas R. Green, "The Catholic Committee for the Ratification of the Child Labor Amendment, 1935-1937: Origin and Limits," *The Catholic Historical Review*, April 1988, pp. 248-269; and Richard B. Sherman, "The Rejection of the Child Labor Amendment," *Mid-America: An Historical Review*, January 1963, pp. 3-17. Sherman analyzes the various factors that contributed to the defeat of the child labor campaign during the 1920s.

[16] Trattner, *Crusade for the Children*, p. 189. See also Irwin Yellowitz, "The Origins of Unemployment Reform," *Labor History*, fall 1968, pp. 354-355.

[17] Margaret H. Schoenfeld, "Analysis of the Labor Provisions of the N.R.A. Codes," *Monthly Labor Review*, March 1935, pp. 59 1-595; Ella Arvilla Merritt, "Trend of Child Labor, 1927-1936," *Monthly Labor Review*, December 1937, pp. 1371-1390.

[18] Trattner, *Crusade for the Children*, pp. 209-2 10; Fred Greenbaum, *Fighting Progressive: A Biography of Edward P. Costigan*, (Washington: Public Affairs Press, 1971), pp. 143-154; and Stuart Jamieson, *Labor Unionism in American Agriculture*, Washington, U.S. Department of Agriculture, Bulletin No. 836, June 1945, pp. 243-244.

[19] Herbert C. Morton, *Public Contracts and Private Wages: Experience Under the Walsh- Healey Act* (Washington: The Brookings Institution, 1965), pp. 14-15, and 23-24. Where government efforts to regulate private sector labor standards had often been disallowed by the courts, setting standards for itself as a consumer had been more successful.

[20] Concerning constitutional issues of this period, see John W. Chambers, "The Big Switch: Justice Roberts and the Minimum-Wage Cases," *Labor History*, winter 1969, pp. 44-73.

[21] Trattner, *Crusade for the Children*, p. 203. See also Storrs, *Civilizing Capitalism*, p. 334.

[22] Frances Perkins, *The Roosevelt I Knew* (New York: The Viking Press, 1946), p. 257.

[23] Although child labor concerns were voiced during debate on the wage/hour legislation, separate hearings were held on that issue. See U.S. Congress, Senate Committee on Interstate Commerce, *To Regulate the Products of Child Labor*, 75th Cong., 1st sess., May 12, 18, and 20, 1937, 192 p.

[24] Jeremy P. Felt, "The Child Labor Provisions of the Fair Labor Standards Act," *Labor History*, fall 1970, pp. 478-479. Jonathan Grossman, then DOL staff historian, similarly notes: "The law avoided some sectors of the work force where most abuses of child labor were concentrated, such as migrant labor, and 'street trades,' such as newspaper venders and shoeshine boys. According to one estimate, only 30,000 child laborers outside of agriculture would be affected." See Jonathan Grossman, "Fair Labor Standards Act of 1938: Maximum Struggle for a Minimum Wage," *Monthly Labor Review*, June 1978, p. 29.

[25] See *GEMSCO, Inc.* v. *Walling*, 324 U.S. 244 (1945).

[26] Section 203(l) defines "oppressive child labor." Section 212 defines the relationship of goods produced by child labor with movement in interstate commerce. Section 213(c) sets forth the specialized treatment of child workers under the act and the pattern of exemptions from otherwise standard coverage. The states may (and normally do) have their own child labor laws. While these may supplement the FLSA, they are not necessarily consistent with the FLSA standard. Where there is overlapping coverage, the higher standard (most protective of the youth worker) will normally prevail. When exploring coverage in any particular case, both the state and federal statutes need to be taken into account.

[27] See Title 29 C.F.R. Part 570 for a more complete explanation of child labor regulation in general. In addition, DOL may have issued "opinion letters" that apply a provision of the FLSA to specific workplaces.

[28] The Department of Labor estimates that, during the late 1990s, about 7% of all farmworkers were between 14 and 17 years of age: that is, about 126,000 children in that age group were employed on American farms. However, an unknown number of youth younger than 14 years of age are also employed in agriculture. See U.S. Department of Labor, *Report on the Youth Labor Force*, pp. 52-53.

[29] As the 1977 FLSA amendments were written, a grower could employ children age 10 and 11 so long as the grower/employer could demonstrate that any pesticides used in the production process would not be harmful for children under 12. Since growers have not been able to demonstrate the harmlessness of such pesticides, they have the choice of (a) not using pesticides or (b) not employing children age 10 or 11. Children 12 years of age or older can be employed.

[30] See 29 C.F.R. § 570.50.

[31] National Committee for Children and Youth, *Social Dynamite: The Report of the Conference on Unemployed, Out-of-School Youth in Urban Areas*, May 24-26, 1961, Washington, 1961, pp. 1-2.

[32] The article, "To Be Young, Black and Out of Work," *The New York Times Magazine*, October 23, 1977, p. 39, stated: "Nearly half of all minority youths between 16 and 19 who are in the work force are unemployed." Similarly, *The AFL-CIO American Federationist*, January 1978, p. 1, in an article by Barbara Becnel, "Black Workers: Progress Derailed," observed that unemployment rates "for black teenagers have reached catastrophic levels. In 1976 they averaged 39.2 percent, and in July 1977 they reached an all-time recorded high of 45.5 percent." See U.S. Congress, Joint Economic Committee, *Youth Unemployment*, hearing,

94th Cong., 2nd sess., September 9, 1976 (Washington: GPO, 1977), 130 p.; and U.S. Congress, Senate Committee on the Budget, *Youth Unemployment*, hearing, 95th Cong., 2nd sess., February 17, 1978 (Washington: GPO, 1978), 136 p.

[33] Concerning employment of workers under 15 years of age, see the collection of essays on youth employment, based on the National Longitudinal Surveys Program of the Bureau of Labor Statistics commencing from 1997 (NLSY97), published in the August 2001 edition of the *Monthly Labor Review*. In their article, "Illegal Child Labor in the United States: Prevalence and Characteristics" (*Industrial and Labor Relations Review*, October 2000, pp. 17-40), Douglas L. Kruse and Douglas Mahony examine this sub-set of youth workers and evaluate the value of currently available data on workers under 15 years of age.

[34] U.S. Department of Labor, *Report on the Youth Labor Force*, updated November 2000, pp. 30-31. Hispanics are included in both black and white data sets. Data are pooled across a three-year period.

[35] Press release from Congressman George Miller, July 27, 1982.

[36] U.S. Congress, House Committee on Education and Labor, Subcommittee on Labor Standards, *Oversight Hearings — Proposed Changes in Child Labor Regulations*, hearing, 97th Cong., 2nd sess., July 28, and August 3, 1982, pp. 1-30.

[37] Peter Edelman, "Child Labor Revisited," *The Nation*, August 21-28, 1982, p. 136.

[38] *Nation's Restaurant News*, February 28, 1983, p. 2.

[39] Bureau of National Affairs, *Daily Labor Report*, April 23, 1984, p. A7.

[40] Ken Rankin, "Pols May Pull Child Labor Scheme off Back Burner," *Nation's Restaurant News*, November 26, 1984, p. 9.

[41] Bureau of National Affairs, *Daily Labor Report*, April 30, 1985, p. A9.

[42] Joseph A. Walsh, "Teen-Age Work Rules Targeted Again," *UA Journal*, September 1982, p. 4.

[43] Bureau of National Affairs, *Daily Labor Report*, May 18, 1989, pp. A10-A1 1. The Committee had addressed such issues as "door-to-door" sales by persons 14 to 15 years of age, a special overtime exemption for "bat boys," and work around commercial paper balers. It also examined the structure of penalties for child labor violations. During this period, GAO was looking into some of these same issues while the National Consumers' League launched its own independent review of child labor practices.

[44] Bureau of National Affairs, *Daily Labor Report*, July 31, 1989, pp. A6-A7; and August 30, 1989, pp. A7-A8.

[45] Bureau of National Affairs, *Daily Labor Report*, November 22, 1989, pp. A7-A8.

[46] Bureau of National Affairs, *Daily Labor Report*, February 8, 1990, pp. A10-A12.

[47] Bureau of National Affairs, *Daily Labor Report*, March 19, 1990, pp. A1 6-A1 7; May 1, 1990, p. A11; and June 26, 1990, pp. A8-A9.

[48] Bureau of National Affairs, *Daily Labor Report*, May 4, 1990, pp. A1 3-A1 5.

[49] Bureau of National Affairs, *Daily Labor Report*, June 25, 1990, p. A8.

[50] Bureau of National Affairs, *Daily Labor Report*, November 5, 1990, pp. A6-A7; and November 13, 1990, p. A6.

[51] *Congressional Record*, April 9, 1986, p. S9013.

[52] *Federal Register*, May 13, 1994, p. 25167; and April 17, 1995, pp. 19336-19337. The basis for the decision is explained by Robert B. Reich in his account, *Locked in the Cabinet* (New York: Alfred A. Knopf, 1997), pp. 113-116.

[53] *Federal Register*, April 17, 1995, p. 19337.

[54] Letter from Karen Keesling to Ronald A. Block (attorney for the National Grocers Association), October 16, 1992.

[55] Statement of Thomas F. Wenning, Senior Vice President and General Counsel, National Grocers Association (NGA), July 11, 1995, House Subcommittee on Workforce Protection.

[56] *Congressional Record*, May 2, 1995, pp. S6009-S6010; October 24, 1995, pp. H10661-H10667; and July 16, 1996, pp. S7912-S7914. See also U.S. Congress, House Committee on Economic and Educational Opportunities, *Authority for 16 and 17 Year Olds to Load*

Materials into Balers and Compactors, report to accompany H.R. 1114, 104th Cong., 1st sess., H.Rept. 104-278 (Washington: GPO, 1995).

57 CRS Report 98-561, *Child Labor in Hazardous Occupations: "On-the-Job Driving" by Youth Workers*, by William G. Whittaker.

58 *Congressional Record*, May 16, 1985, p. E2251.

59 Statement of Susan R. Meisinger, Deputy Under Secretary for Employment Standards, DOL, November 6, 1985, the House Judiciary Subcommittee on Civil and Constitutional Rights.

60 Statement of Victoria Toensing, Deputy Assistant Attorney General, Criminal Division, November 6, 1985, the House Judiciary Subcommittee on Civil and Constitutional Rights.

61 U.S. Congress, Senate Committee on Governmental Affairs. Permanent Subcommittee on Investigations, *Exploitation of Young Adults in Door-to-Door Sales*, hearing, 100th Cong., 1st sess., April 6, 1987, 217 p.

62 U.S. Congress, House Committee on Government Operations, Subcommittee on Employment and Housing, *Children at Risk in the Workplace*, hearing, 101st Cong., 2nd sess., March 16, June 8, 1990, pp. 277-297.

63 The issue, however defined, continued to arise periodically. See Jim Naughton, "Children's Candy Sales Are Criticized: Distributors Under Scrutiny for Possible Child Labor Infractions," *The Washington Post*, May 9, 1990, pp. A1, A10; "State Trying To Close Down Firm Employing Youngsters," *The Daily Olympian*, October 15, 1990, pp. C1 - C2; and Julie Barrett, "Kiddie Hawkers," *Generation Next*, July/August 1995, pp. 22-23.

64 *Congressional Record*, November 19, 1999, p. S15 102.

65 A somewhat condensed version of the legislation (H.R. 3070) was introduced in the House during the 107th Congress by Representative Thomas Petri (R-WI). No action was taken on the Petri bill.

66 *Congressional Record*, August 1, 2002, p. S8022.

67 *Congressional Record*, September 24, 2003, pp. E1 873-E1 874.

68 See 29 C.F.R. §§ 570.54 and 750.55. In a letter of July 22, 1998, to Chairman William F. Goodling (R-PA), then-Chair of the Committee on Education and the Workforce, Deputy Secretary of Labor Kathryn Higgins explained the special hazards associated with work in the lumber and wood products industry which, she said, were "exacerbated for youth" given their "lack of training" and "immaturity."

69 Bureau of National Affairs, *Daily Labor Report*, July 23, 1998, p. A11. Concerning the Amish perspective on public education, see Gertrude Enders Huntington, "Persistence and Change in Amish Education," in Donald B. Kraybill and Marc A. Olshan (eds.), *The Amish Struggle with Modernity* (Hanover, New Hampshire: University Press of New England, 1994), pp.77-95; and Thomas J. Meyers, "Education and Schooling," in Kraybill (ed.), *The Amish and the State* (Baltimore: The Johns Hopkins University Press, 2003), pp. 87-106.

70 Steven Greenhouse, "Foes of Idle Hands, Amish Contest a Child Labor Law," *The New York Times*, October 18, 2003, p. A1.

71 Ibid. The issue involves sons, not daughters. Greenhouse explains, p. 9, "Teenage girls, as always, learn skills like quilting or work in retail shops." See also Marc A. Olshan and Kimberly D. Schmidt, "Amish Women and the Feminist Conundrum," in Kraybill and Olshan (eds.), pp. 215-230.

72 *Congressional Record*, September 28, 1998, pp. H9121-H9124. See also U.S. Congress, House Committee on Education and the Workforce, Subcommittee on Workforce Protections, *The Effect of the Fair Labor Standards Act on Amish Families and H.R. 2038, the MSPA Clarification Act*, hearing, 105th Cong., 2nd sess., April 21, 1998 (Washington: GPO, 1998); and U.S. Congress, House Committee on Education and the Workforce, *Amending the Fair Labor Standards Act of 1938 To Permit Certain Youth To Perform Certain Work with Wood Products*, report together with minority views to accompany H.R. 221, H.Rept. 106-31, 106th Cong., 1st sess., (Washington: GPO, 1999), 29 p.

73 The issue of school attendance is developed in some detail in *Wisconsin v. Yoder*, 406 U.S. 205 (1972).

[74] The proposed legislation deals narrowly with employment of children in sawmills and related woodworking establishments. Their employment in other fields, currently restricted by law or by administrative ruling, would require separate action.

[75] Jennifer Brown, "Old Ways Persevere, Flourish: Non-Mainstream Culture Helps Anabaptist Communities Retain Hold on the Young," *The Washington Post*, April 21, 2001, p. B9.

[76] These issues are discussed in Joel Feinberg, "The Child's Right to an Open Future," in William Aiken and Hugh LaFollette (eds.), *Whose Child? Children's Rights, Parental Authority, and State Power* (Totowa, N.J.: Rowman and Littlefield, 1980), pp. 124-153; and Dena S. Davis, "The Child's Right to an Open Future: *Yoder* and Beyond," *Capital University Law Review*, vol. 26 (1997), pp. 93-105. See also Albert N. Keim (ed.), *Compulsory Education and the Amish: The Right Not to Be Modern* (Boston: Beacon Press, 1975).

[77] Testimony of Rep. Mark Souder before the Senate Subcommittee on Labor, Health and Human Services and Education, Committee on Appropriations, May 3, 2001.

[78] Testimony of Thomas M. Markey, Acting Administrator, Wage and Hour Division, U.S. Department of Labor, before the Subcommittee on Labor, Health and Human Services, and Education, Committee on Appropriations, U.S. Senate, May 3, 2001.

[79] *Congressional Record*, June 13, 2001, pp. S6153-S6154.

[80] The wording is from S. 974. The phrasing of H.R. 1943 is slightly different.

[81] Opening statement of Chairman Norwood, October 8, 2003.

[82] Testimony of Rep. Pitts, October 8, 2003.

[83] Testimony of Rep. Souder, October 8, 2003.

[84] Testimony of Christ K. Blank, Chairman, Voice of the Old Order Amish, Old Order Amish Steering Committee, October 8, 2003.

[85] Testimony of Nicholas Clark, October 8, 2003. Clark stated: "The proposal would also require government investigators to determine whether owners of firms seeking to employ child labor, and their child employees, are truly Amish. Such determinations would necessarily entangle the government in the practice of religion, also in violation of the First Amendment."

[86] *Congressional Record*, December 8, 2003, p. 12845.

[87] U.S. Congress, Conference Committees, *Making Appropriations for Agriculture, Rural Development, Food and Drug Administration, and Related Agencies for the Fiscal Year Ending September 30, 2004, and for Other Purposes*, conference report to accompany H.R. 2673, 108th Cong., 1st sess., H.Rept. 108-401 (Washington, GPO, 2003), pp. 734 and 235-236. See also *DLR* December 3, 2003, pp. A1 1-A12.

[88] *Congressional Record*, January 22, 2004, pp. S155-S 156.

[89] Press release, Office of Senator Arlen Specter, January 23, 2004, the Senator's website, visited on January 29, 2004.

[90] *Congressional Record*, September 18, 2002, pp. H6349-H6350.

[91] This is a general summary of the provisions of H.R. 1142. The reader may want to review the text of the bill for more precision and detail.

[92] This is a general summary of the provisions of H.R. 2870. The reader may want to review the text of the bill for more precision and detail.

[93] A "serious work-related injury" is one that results in "(1) the death of the minor; (2) medical attention for the minor; or (3) investigation by a law enforcement agency."

[94] Arguably, the latter could include protection of child models. See discussion above.

INDEX

D

E

R

S

T

U

V

W

Y